I0520590

Kings Among Men

RANDALL J. BREWER

CONTENTS

Copyright © 2025 by Randall J. Brewer
All rights reserved. No part of this book may be reproduced in any
manner whatsoever without written permission except in the case of
brief quotations embodied in critical articles and reviews.
First Printing, 2025

KINGS AMONG MEN

INTRODUCTION

From the very beginning, God's intent for man was never survival - it was rulership. In the book of Genesis, before sin, before failure, before the curse, God placed Adam in the garden and gave him dominion. That word "dominion" means authority, rulership, sovereignty. It was Heaven's declaration that man was not created to be a slave to circumstances, sin, or systems, but to govern life under the leadership of his Creator. Every man was fashioned in the image of a King, designed to reflect Heaven's order upon the earth.

But sin disrupted that divine order. When Adam fell, man lost his crown. He exchanged authority for shame, rulership for survival, purpose for existence. Since then, generation after generation of men have wandered through life trying to recover what was lost - identity, purpose, significance. Yet deep inside, the cry of kingship remains. Every man feels it. It's that unexplainable pull toward greatness, that desire to build, to lead, to protect, to leave a legacy that outlives him. It's the echo of Eden—the royal DNA of God still pulsing within the heart of His sons.

When Jesus came, He did not come merely to forgive sins; He came to restore a Kingdom. He came to reestablish man's dominion under God's authority. "Fear not, little flock," He said, "for it is your Father's good pleasure to give you the Kingdom" (Luke 12:32). The cross wasn't just a place of redemption; it was the gateway back to kingship. Through Christ, man regains access to his royal inheritance. He is no longer a victim of his past or a servant to sin; he is a king and priest unto God (Revelation 1:6).

This truth changes everything. The call to kingship is not reserved for a select few - it is the divine destiny of every man who names the name of Christ. Whether you are a husband, father, pastor, business owner, or laborer, God has placed within you the capacity to reign in life through Jesus Christ (Romans 5:17). To reign means to influence, to govern, to bring order where there is chaos, and to represent Heaven's authority wherever you stand.

The tragedy of our generation is that many men have forgotten who they are. They have settled for comfort instead of calling, passivity instead of power. They live as peasants when God has called them to be kings. Society may tell you that masculinity is outdated, that manhood is toxic, that leadership is arrogance, but the Word of God says otherwise. True kingship is not domination; it is servanthood. It is strength under submission. It is the willingness to lead through love, to guide through wisdom, and to build through faith.

This book is a call to awaken the king within you. It is an invitation to rediscover your royal identity and to walk boldly in the authority Christ has restored. You were not created to merely exist; you were born to reign. The same God who called David from the fields, Joseph from the prison, and Gideon from the winepress is calling you to step into your destiny as a king in His kingdom.

Every chapter will challenge you to see yourself differently - to rise from the dust of mediocrity and take your rightful place as a man of purpose, integrity, and vision. You will learn that ruling begins with responsibility, that leadership flows from humility, and that true kingship is measured not by how many serve you, but by how many you serve.

The kingdom of God needs men who will stand up again, men who understand that authority without submission leads to destruction, but submission under divine authority releases power. It needs men who will govern their homes with grace, their minds with truth, and their hearts with purity. It needs men who will walk in the wisdom of Solomon, the courage of David, and the faith of Abraham.

The time for passivity is over. The days of confusion about manhood must end. God is calling His sons to rise, to reclaim their crowns, to rule their spheres, and to reflect His glory in every arena of life. You were not born to chase success; you were born to manifest dominion. You were not born to blend in; you were born to stand out as a representative of Heaven's rule on the earth.

You are a king in God's kingdom. Not tomorrow. Not someday. Today. Open your heart, sharpen your mind, and prepare to see yourself the way God sees you. Because once you discover who you truly are in Christ, you'll never settle for less than the throne He's called you to occupy.

Welcome to your royal awakening.

| 1 |

"YOU ARE A KING"

All men are called to be kings in the kingdom of God. Rev. 1:6 says Jesus Christ "has made us kings and priests to His God and Father, to Him be glory and dominion forever and ever. Amen." Every man born of God is not just saved; he's called to reign as a king. You were never meant to live defeated and broken lives, or to be uncertain of your purpose. From the very beginning, God's intention was for His sons to walk in dominion; to rule with righteousness, to lead with love, and to influence the world through the power of His Spirit. When you came into Christ, you didn't just receive forgiveness; you received a crown. You became part of a royal bloodline. Your Father is the King of Heaven, and He expects His sons to walk with authority, integrity, and purpose. Kings are men whose job it is to represent God and His kingdom on the earth. Your appointment as a king is divine. You weren't chosen by casting of votes. You are a king because you are the son of a King.

You are somebody special. You are not worthless or insignificant. You are a king! You are the righteousness of God in

Christ Jesus (2 Cor. 5:21). Being a king in God's kingdom means serving with strength. It means standing firm in truth when others bow to compromise. It means protecting what God has entrusted to you - your family, your faith, your calling - and ruling with wisdom, courage, and compassion. Every challenge you face is an opportunity to prove your kingship. Every battle is a chance to show that you trust the One who sits on the throne. You are not ordinary. You are chosen. You are royal. You are a king under the great King, a man called to advance God's kingdom on the earth. You were called out of darkness into His marvelous light so stand up and shout from the rooftop, "I AM A KING!" Now rise up. Adjust your crown. Take your place. Rule with righteousness. For the world is waiting to see what a true man of God - a true king - looks like.

Every Christian man must understand his divine identity. You are more than you think you are. You are a king! You are not just a believer, you are a son of God, born into His royal family. Through Christ, you've been given authority to rule and reign in life, not through pride or power, but through righteousness and faith. You are royalty! You are not to be ruled over but to rule. Satan doesn't want you to know this. He wants you to live in fear, poverty, lack, and want. But when you know who you are in Christ, that you're the head and not the tail, above and not beneath (Deut. 28:13), that He has made you a king, you will never be defeated again. So walk with confidence. Speak with faith. Stand firm in your purpose. The world needs to see sons of God who know who they are. They need to see men who lead with strength, humility, and heavenly authority. You are royalty. You are chosen. You are called to rule in life for the glory of your Father.

1 John 4:4 says, "Greater is He who is in me than he who is in the world." You are a king because the King is living in you. There is royalty flowing in your veins. God's power in you causes you to triumph over every situation, every obstacle, every setback (2 Cor. 2:14). Rom. 5:17 declares, "Those who receive abundance of grace and of the gift of righteousness will reign in life through the One, Christ Jesus." That means you were never meant to live defeated or powerless lives. You carry the King's name, the King's Spirit, and the King's authority and nothing can block your progress as you set out to fulfill your destiny. So walk with confidence. Speak with faith. Stand firm in your purpose. The world needs to see sons of God who know who they are. They need to see men who lead with strength, humility, and heavenly authority. You are royalty. You are chosen. You are called to rule in life for the glory of your Father.

As a king, you have access to everything the kingdom has to offer. You have access to every blessing, every gift, every promise, every provision. You have access to the abundance of God's grace, His peace, His love, His joy, His power, His authority. You can eat at the King's table as one of His sons all the days of your life. You are not a beggar; you are an heir. You don't have to strive for what has already been given to you through Christ. When you were born again, you were born into royalty. The King of kings adopted you, crowned you, and gave you access to everything His kingdom holds. As a king in God's kingdom, you can come boldly to the throne of grace whenever you want to (Heb. 4:16). You were not called to live beneath your privilege because all of heaven's resources are at your disposal, things such as wisdom, strength, favor, provision, and authority.

It is in God's presence where kings rule and reign. The same Spirit that raised Him from the dead lives inside you, empowering you to walk in dominion and victory. God prepared a place for Adam to dwell in and work in. God's presence was in that place (Gen. 3:8). Like a fish out of water, kings cannot operate successfully outside of God's presence. God has a place for every king to reign, a place for a king to succeed, a place for a king to work. That place is in His divine presence. This is why He invites you to eat at the King's table. Kings don't ask permission to take hold of what belongs to them; they simply exercise their right to have what is theirs. You are seated with Christ in heavenly places, far above the powers of darkness (Eph. 2:6). So lift your head up high, son of the King. You are royalty. You have access. Everything in the Kingdom is yours, because you belong to the King who owns it all.

God is looking for a few good men, those fueled by a relentless pursuit of becoming a wholehearted man, of becoming a king in God's kingdom. Every man of God carries within him the seed of kingship. You were created to lead, to influence, to protect, and to establish the rule of Heaven in the earth. God is searching for men who will rule not by pride or power, but by righteousness, humility, and wisdom. The world may be full of pretenders, but God's Kingdom is calling for true kings - men after His own heart. Step forward. Take your place. Walk in your authority. You were born to be great, and you were born to be a king. The path to becoming a king is a narrow path and you must seek with all diligence ways to fulfill your God-given role. God is looking for men who will step forward in faith and become kings in the kingdom. He is not looking for men who shrink back in fear. He is looking for men who understand that they were not born to blend in but to reign with Christ.

Before a man can wear the crown, he must first bow before the throne because true kingship begins in surrender. God has placed you on the path that leads to becoming a king and He expects you to walk on that path. Jer. 6:16 says, "Stand in the ways and see, and ask for the old paths, where the good way is, and walk in it; Then you will find rest for your souls." There is no fast, easy way to become a king. You must work to become who you are. It's the process of inner transformation that leads to the type of legacy all men dream of. The journey down this narrow path will require courage, vulnerability, and a determination to never give up. Men who become kings are those who are thirsty for adventure, those who are willing to go beyond the norm. They'll do whatever it takes because they know being a king in God's kingdom is the only way their masculine soul will flourish.

The greatest need in the world today is not more politicians, programs, or possessions - it is for kings who live on the earth but rule from the perspective of heaven. A cry of desperation is going out for kings to be manifested on the earth today. The earth groans under the weight of confusion, compromise, and corruption. Nations are searching for direction, but true leadership does not come from human wisdom - it comes from those who have been seated with Christ in heavenly places. These are the men who understand that their authority is not earthly but divine. The world needs you. It needs ordinary men whose hearts have found life, meaning, and purpose with an extraordinary God. This is the hour for the manifestation of kingdom kings - godly men who carry heaven's authority into the systems of the world. They are not driven by pride or power but by purpose. They reign not for themselves but for the glory of God.

The world needs men who know who they are in Christ, men who reclaim their identity, strength, integrity, and their God-given purpose. They need men who will walk the narrow path, men who will get out on a limb and risk moving toward the call of kingship. They're looking for the type of man to whom God greatly delights to entrust the care of His kingdom. The absence of kings is bringing destruction, pain, and anguish throughout the land. Families, churches, and communities break down when there is no influence of a king. Without kings in the society, there will be chaos and confusion all over. Now is the time for the kings of the Kingdom to take their rightful place - to live on earth, but rule from heaven. When heaven's kings rise, darkness must bow. When heaven's kings speak, truth is revealed. When heaven's kings rule, peace returns. If men don't rise up and become kings, God said in Mal. 4:6 that He will "come and strike the earth with a curse."

There is a cry echoing through the earth - a cry for kings. It rises from the chaos of the world, from the hearts of men, and even from the throne of Almighty God Himself. Yes, even God Himself is crying out. He said in Ezekiel 22:30 "So I sought for a man among them who would make a wall and stand in the gap before Me on behalf of the land, that I should not destroy it; but I found no one." Ten righteous men couldn't be found in Sodom and Gomorrah, and the two cities were destroyed with fire and brimstone. A curse on the land is the result of a lack of kings in the world. God said in Is. 3:12, "As for My people, children are their oppressors, and women rule over them." Cultures are destroyed when children become oppressors and women do the ruling. Is. 3:12 continues, "O My people! Those who lead you cause you to err and destroy the way of your paths." Cultures disintegrate when men don't fulfill their role as kings.

The world is longing for righteous leadership, for men who will stand tall with conviction and integrity. Creation itself is yearning for sons who will take their rightful place - not as tyrants or oppressors, but as kings under the rule of the King of kings. Men, too, are crying out - whether they realize it or not. Deep within every man is a longing to walk in divine purpose, to rule well over what God has entrusted to him: his home, his calling, his territory. Yet many have forgotten who they are. They've laid down their crowns for comfort, traded their authority for acceptance, and lost sight of the divine mandate placed upon them from the beginning - to have dominion, to lead with love, and to reflect the heart of God. This is the cry of Heaven - a search for men who will rise as kings and priests, who will intercede for the land, who will rebuild the broken walls, and who will stand unwavering in the face of darkness. The time for passive manhood is over. The earth is calling. Heaven is calling. God is calling.

God sets kings in the midst of all the chaos and confusion that's on the earth today. Therefore, it is now time for the kings to arise - men of courage, conviction, and compassion who will rule not for their glory, but for His. In the midst of worldly chaos, when nations tremble, economies shake, and men's hearts fail them for fear - true men of God rise up and never retreat. They are not subject to the instability of this world for they are kings and priests unto God. It is in the midst of all this turmoil that kings rule and reign. It's where they manage life according to the rule book God has given them, the Holy Bible. Kings do not panic when storms arise - they rule through them. They do not bow to fear - they decree peace, purpose, and order according to Heaven's will. The world may be in turmoil, but the Kingdom of God is not. Christ is still on the throne, and we reign with Him.

Before the fall, Adam was the prototype of what a kingly man was created to be. In Gen.1, when God created the heavens and the earth, over and over again it says, "Then God said...Then God said...Then God said..." But something changed in chapter two when He formed man. Over and over again it says "the Lord God" did this and "the Lord God" did that. In chapter one He was the powerful God, in chapter two He was the re-lational Lord God. The word "lord" means 'master; owner.' If you are a lord, you have the right to tell somebody what to do. You are not a king unless God is your Lord, unless He is telling you what to do. Notice carefully what happened when the devil showed up in the Garden of Eden. The serpent asked the woman, "Has God indeed said, 'You shall not eat of every tree of the garden'?" (Gen. 3:1). What's missing here? The devil said the word "God" and not "Lord God."

He was telling Eve that God did not have the authority to tell her what to do. What's more, when Eve responded to the serpent, she also said the word "God" (Gen. 3:3) and not "Lord God." She was agreeing with Satan that God was not Lord, that He did not have the right or authority to tell her what to do. Chaos comes when God is not allowed to be Lord in the life of a man. What is a king? A king is a man who has learned to live his life under the lordship of Jesus Christ. A king understands that he is obligated to a higher order. The goal of a king is to implement the rule of God, not create his own rules along the way. When God created Adam, He was Yahweh Elohim. He was the powerful Lord God who wants to relate to you and have the final say in your life. God's kingdom on the earth is the visible manifestation of the comprehensive rule of God over all of life. A man who is a king operates under the lordship of God.

A king is a man whose God is also his Lord, the One who oversees the affairs of his life. When men become independent from God, they become their own king. This makes them a competitor with the Lord God. Pain and anguish come to a king and his kingdom when he refuses to do what God tells him to do. From Saul's defiance to David's moment of failure,

Scripture reminds us that no one is too powerful to fall, and no kingdom is too strong to crumble when God's commands are ignored. Obedience brings blessing, but rebellion opens the door to sorrow. When God gives a word, He expects action. And when He gives an order, He expects obedience - not excuses, not hesitation, not pride. For every king who refuses to bow to the King of Kings, pain and anguish will reign where peace once ruled. Indeed, there is only room for one high King in the world. His name is Jesus, the King of kings and Lord of lords. A king knows that God has the last and final say. Always!

| 2 |

"BECOMING A KING"

God is opening before you a divine opportunity - the chance to reign with Him. Not in the way the world seeks power, but in the way Heaven defines greatness. You have been chosen, set apart, and called to rise into your royal identity in Christ. Through His grace, God is making available to you the authority, wisdom, and anointing of a king in His Kingdom. This isn't about earthly crowns or thrones - it's about spiritual rulership, divine responsibility, and kingdom influence. When you walk in obedience, faith, and humility, God positions you to rule over circumstances instead of being ruled by them. He equips you to lead with righteousness, justice, and love - reflecting the heart of the true King, Jesus Christ. Now is the time to step into your calling. The King of kings is inviting you to take your place - to rule with integrity, to reign in righteousness, and to expand His Kingdom on earth as it is in Heaven.

Becoming a king isn't easy and it isn't quick but, for sure, it will be worth the cost. The best things in life are. Out in front of you is a life of deep meaning, adventure, beauty, courage, and intimate relationships. Be willing to step forward and go after it for it is truly a life worth fighting for. Get out of the boat and risk taking one more step into the unknown. Become the king you were born to be. To become a king requires soul-centered honesty, courage, and love. Recovering the fullness of what it means to bear the image of God is central to the transformation of being a man into becoming a king. One of the greatest treasures given to man by the heart of God is the restoration of their true identity, to become who they are known as in God's kingdom. Becoming that man is the most rare, the most remarkable, and the most holy journey you will ever take. As you step onto that narrow path of becoming a king, you'll come to know what God sees when He looks at you.

Many men want to be matadors until they find themselves in a ring with a 2000-pound bull staring at them. It's then that they realize what they really wanted is to wear tight pants and hear the roar of the crowd. The reality of becoming what you want may not be as glamorous as it may first appear. This why you need gut-like determination to go deep inside you. Becoming a king in God's Kingdom isn't for the faint of heart. It takes more than talent, more than opportunity, and more than good intentions - it takes guts. True kingship in the Spirit is forged through trials, perseverance, and a heart that refuses to quit when the pressure mounts. David wasn't crowned because of comfort; he was chosen because of courage. Before he ever wore a crown, he faced lions, bears, and giants - not just in the field, but in his soul. It was his gut-like determination to trust God no matter what that prepared him for the throne.

Every man called by God must develop that same holy grit - the inner resolve to keep moving forward when everything in you wants to give up. It's the kind of faith that stands tall in the valley, that keeps swinging the sling even when the giant looks unbeatable. God is raising up kings who don't run from adversity but rise through it. Men who have learned that pain is not a signal to quit - it's the birthplace of purpose. If you want to rule with Christ, you must be willing to fight like David, endure like Joseph, and believe like Abraham. Kings are not made in comfort; they're formed in conflict. Let God draw out of you the man you're supposed to be. Dig deep. Stand firm. And let that gut-like determination drive you toward your destiny. Listen carefully because every day God is whispering in your ear, telling you who you were born to be and what His intentions for your life are.

God said in Jer. 1:5 (MSG), "Before I shaped you in the womb, I knew all about you." Likewise, God knew you before you were born. You, also, need to know who you are. You need close encounters with God that will bring this revelation to light. Draw near to God and make sure the number one goal in your life is to become the king you were born to be. Not a king who rules over people, but one who reigns in purpose, discipline, and faith. God created you with royal potential, and every trial, every lesson, every victory is shaping you into the man He designed you to become. Don't settle for mediocrity when you were born for greatness. Walk with integrity, lead with humility, and serve with love. Rise up and conquer fear, doubt, and sin, because a true king rules first over himself. The crown you seek is a crown of righteousness that comes from living according to God's will. Your destiny is not in fame or fortune, but in fulfilling the divine purpose for which you were born.

Throughout Scripture, we see that when God changes a person's name, He is also changing their identity, purpose, and destiny. Abram became Abraham. No longer was he just "exalted father," but "father of many nations." Sarai became Sarah, a mother of kings. And Saul, once a persecutor of Christians, became Paul, a preacher to the nations. When God gives you a new name, He's declaring who you are in His kingdom, not who you were in your past. Your old name represented limitation, fear, and mistakes but your new name carries divine purpose, authority, and identity. Begin to believe who you truly are, and who you're to be known in God's kingdom. You cannot step into your new assignment with your old identity. God is calling you higher, giving you a name that matches your mission. Receive the new name God wants to bestow on you. Your new name is "King!"

There comes a time in every believer's journey when God calls us beyond who we've been, to embrace who He created us to be. God desires to speak into your spirit and reveal who you truly are in His eyes - not what the world has called you, not what your past has labeled you, but what Heaven declares over you. In the words of George MacDonald, "Since we are, so must we become." When a man encounters the living God in the depths of his soul, he is given a new identity, a new name. A new name expresses the character and the nature of the man who bears it. It is the man's own symbol, his soul's picture in a word. A man's new name is the picture of who and what he is intended to become. A man's journey in life is to become what his name says he is to become. So today, open your heart to receive the new name God wants to bestow on you. He's not just changing what people call you; He's changing who you are.

Jesus said in Rev. 2:17, "To him who overcomes, to him I will give a white stone, and a new name written on the stone." This verse is a powerful reminder that God rewards those who remain steadfast and faithful to Him through every trial. The white stone represents purity, victory, and acceptance - an emblem of divine approval. In ancient times, a white stone was often given to those acquitted in court or to victors in games, symbolizing honor and belonging. The new name written on it speaks of a personal relationship with God; something unique, intimate, and eternal. It represents transformation and identity in Christ. When we overcome the battles of life through faith, we are not just surviving; we are being reshaped into who God destined us to be. The color white is not what's being referred to here. The Greek word "leukos" means 'to shine like the sun.' It is the Greek word used to describe the transfiguration of Jesus. It refers to a bright, glowing light that is not of this world.

To the overcomer, God gives not just a reward, but a reminder that you are known, chosen, and redeemed. Your identity is not in your past or your struggle; it's in the name He gives you. The Greek word for "stone" is "psephor" and it means 'eternal; permanent; something that can't be taken away.' The white stone is a symbol of what's inside a man's soul, the man God made him to be. The giving of the white stone with the new name is the communication of what God thinks about the man. Who is this special name given to? The one who overcomes. God wants every man to know he is an overcomer. You are a victorious one. That's part of your name in heaven. Keep overcoming. Keep pushing away the belief that you are a nobody in this world but grasp onto the fact that you are a king in God's kingdom. Step into your destiny knowing your stone awaits, and with it, your new name known only to you and the One who loves you beyond measure.

Two questions must be asked as you strive for wholeheartedness. "Who have I become?" and "Who am I becoming?" The answer to these questions is so important because you cannot live beyond the identity you have embraced. Your life will always rise or fall to the level of who you believe you are. Are you a poor wretched sinner or are you the righteousness of God in Christ Jesus? Are you a slave to the world or a king in God's kingdom? When God changes your name, He's not just changing what people call you; He's changing what Heaven calls you. He's giving you a new identity, a new nature, and a new destiny. But that new life cannot manifest until you embrace that new name. Abram couldn't become the father of many nations until he accepted being called Abraham. Jacob could not walk in destiny until he received his new name Israel, the one who prevails with God. Saul couldn't fulfill his calling until he became Paul, a servant and apostle of Jesus Christ.

If you don't like what you've become, then dismantle the bad and partner with God to restore your true self, the man He cre-

KINGS AMONG MEN - 21

ated you to be. God may have already declared who you are - a mighty man of valor, a chosen vessel, a light to the nations. But if you still see yourself as the old you, you'll live beneath your divine potential. Heaven can call you "redeemed," but if you keep calling yourself "broken," your life will echo the name you answer to. To live the life God has ordained, you must embrace the name God has given you. Align your thoughts, your words, and your expectations with your divine identity. Stop living from who you were and start living from who God says you are. Why? Because you cannot live beyond the identity you have embraced, and you cannot embrace what you refuse to believe. The masculine journey is an ongoing process of putting to death those false names and clinging to the new name God has given you.

If you know and believe you are a king, then act like one. Your actions reveal what you believe one hundred percent of the time. It's what you do every day, day in and day out, that reveals what you really believe about yourself. Never forget that you are unique, a reflecting image of God. Eph. 2:10 (NLT) says, "We are God's masterpiece. He has created us anew in Christ Jesus, so we can do the good things He planned for us long ago." This is one of the most profound truths in all of Scripture. It reminds us that we are not accidents; we are God's workmanship. The word "workmanship" in the Greek is "poiema" from which we get the word "poem." That means you are God's masterpiece, His work of art, carefully designed and beautifully crafted. God didn't just create you to exist; He created you for a divine purpose. Before you ever took your first breath, He already prepared the good works you were meant to walk in. Your life is not random; it's part of God's intentional design.

You need deep-seeded insight and confidence in the person you are on the inside. Strive daily to bring to the world the person you truly are, the person God called you to be. Believe that no matter what circumstances you find yourself in, you're still able to make this world a better place. As a king, you are to live above your circumstances so you can bring the man you are into the world you live in. God is inviting you to be transformed, to become the masterpiece He created you to be. Seek His will. It is only in seeking that we find, in knocking that the door is opened. Give God your consent to have His way in your life. Have a kingdom view of what life is all about. Be encouraged knowing you are God's masterpiece, designed for God's purpose, empowered by God's grace to fulfill God's plan. Walk boldly in the good works He has already prepared for you. Remember, you can't live beyond your identity, the person you see when you look in the mirror.

When God gives you a new name, He's not just changing what people call you - He's revealing who you're meant to become. A divine name is not a label; it's a calling. It speaks to the potential God sees within you long before you see it yourself. Abram became Abraham, "the father of many nations," long before he held a single child in his arms. Jacob became Israel, "the one who wrestles with God," only after facing his own weakness and clinging to the Lord for blessing. Simon became Peter, "the rock," even while he was still unstable and unsure. Each of them received a name that pointed to their destiny but it took time, faith, and obedience to *become* that name. God's new name over your life is an invitation into transformation. It's not a finished statement; it's a prophetic declaration of what He will shape you into as you walk with Him. Because with God, a name isn't just a description - it's a destiny.

The Bible says you are fearfully and wonderfully made (Ps. 139:14). In other words, you are God's greatest work. You are a one-of-a-kind masterpiece crafted by the Master's hands with a supernatural quality added to it. Oswald Chambers said, "It is not what a man does that is of final importance, but what he is in what he does." Is. 62:2 (MSG) says, "You'll get a brand-new name straight from the mouth of God." When God renames you, when He calls you a king, don't just wear the name, grow into it. Let it challenge you. Let it stretch you. Let it remind you of who you are becoming through His grace. Yes, God has a name for you. It's a picture of who you are, a picture of who you are to become. Getting a new name from God is intended to engage you in a process of becoming that name. This name is given to strengthen you and to bring you closer to God, to put you on the path he predestined you to take. Allow this name to be the fuel that propels you forward to becoming all you were called to be.

God said in Jer. 1:5 (MSG), "Before you saw the light of day, I had holy plans for you." There is a reason God wants you to become a king. There is something God wants to bring to the world through you, something nobody else can do but you. Is. 49:1 (MSG) says, "God put me to work from the day I was born. The moment I entered the world He named me." Your new name will help you carry the mantle God intended you to carry. After Paul received his new name, he went away and for almost fourteen years you hear no mention of his name in scripture. He entered into a season of training, a season of becoming that new name. The man who emerged is the man who wrote most of the New Testament. What is your true name? Let God call you what He will. That name makes you the type of person who has nothing to hide, nothing to fear, and nothing to prove.

| 3 |

"CREATED TO DOMINATE"

The message of the Bible is about a King and a kingdom. Jesus never came to bring us religion; He came to restore kings and to deliver to the earth a kingdom. If you can understand that you can understand the entire Bible. From the beginning, God's intent was for man to rule the earth under His authority. He said in Gen. 1:26, "Let them have dominion over the earth." Then came Jesus. He was the Son of God, but also the Son of Man, and He came to reclaim what Adam forfeited. He came not only to redeem us from sin but to restore us to our rightful position as kings and priests unto God (Rev. 1:6).

He came declaring, "Repent, for the Kingdom of heaven is at hand." That was a royal announcement. The King had returned, and His Kingdom was breaking into the world through Him. Everywhere Jesus went, He demonstrated the reality of that Kingdom, healing the sick, casting out demons, restoring the broken, and proclaiming liberty to the captives. These were the acts of a King reclaiming His territory.

Jesus was always preaching about the kingdom (Matt. 4:17; Matt. 4:23; Matt. 5:3; Matt. 6:33). Jesus taught parables about the kingdom (Matt. 13:24; Matt. 13:31; Matt. 25:1; Matt. 25:14). What did Jesus say your top priority should be? "Seek first the kingdom of God and His righteousness" (Matt. 6:33). He taught us to pray, "Thy kingdom come, Thy will be done, on earth as it is in heaven" (Matt. 6:10). The first thing Jesus mentioned in this prayer is the kingdom of God. It was His top priority, and it should be your top priority as well. The Kingdom of God is not a faraway realm; it is a present reality wherever His people live under His lordship and advance His will on earth as it is in Heaven. You were not saved just to escape hell; you were redeemed to restore Heaven's order on earth. Jesus came to restore kings and to deliver to the earth a heavenly kingdom. And now, the crown He wore is the one He places upon His people.

To seek first the Kingdom of God is more than a command. It's an invitation into alignment with heaven. Jesus wasn't telling us to chase blessings, but to pursue God's heart, His ways, and His order. When you seek the values of God, you learn what matters most to Him. Seeking first the kingdom of God is when you connect with Him in such a way that you purpose in your heart to put His will above your own. When you adopt His values, your heart begins to beat in rhythm with His. To seek His kingdom is to unlearn the world's methods and walk in divine wisdom. It means you always put God's interests first. When you make God's Kingdom our first pursuit - not comfort, not status, not material things - you will discover that everything else you need flows naturally out of that relationship. Seeking the Kingdom is not just about going to heaven one day, it's about living under heaven's rule right now.

True success in life doesn't come from luck, talent, or connections, it comes from living according to God's principles. The Bible is full of instructions on how the kingdom of God operates. It is not just a book of stories; it's a divine manual for victorious living. Every principle in God's Word reveals how to walk in wisdom, favor, and fruitfulness. It is not enough to simply know what God says, you must do what He says. When you apply His Word daily, His principles begin to shape your thoughts, guide your actions, and open doors of blessing that no man can shut. Make reading the Word a priority so you can deepen your walk with God. Apply to your life what the Bible tells you so you can be an influence on others. Seek first to discover God's principles for succeeding in life and do what the Bible tells you to do. Seek first His kingdom and His righteousness. Righteousness is having a right standing or positioning with God. It's knowing where you stand with God and being in a good relationship with Him.

From the beginning of time, God's intention was not merely to populate the earth with people but to extend His heavenly kingdom into the visible world. Heaven was meant to be the pattern, Earth, the reflection. God desired to fill the earth with His glory, to see His will carried out here just as it is in Heaven. When He created man in His image, He gave humanity the divine assignment of dominion, to have rulership under His authority. Man was designed to be God's representative, governing the physical realm as Heaven governs the spiritual.

Earth was never meant to operate apart from Heaven's influence; it was meant to be an extension of it. Though sin disrupted that plan, it did not destroy it. Through Jesus Christ, the bridge between Heaven and Earth has been restored. In Him, God's original purpose continues; to fill the earth with citizens of His Kingdom who carry His presence, express His nature, and advance His will.

God's vision remains the same today: that His invisible Kingdom would once again be made visible through His people on Earth. His ultimate goal is to release His influence into the world. The incarnation of Jesus Christ was God coming to the earth as a King. The wise men heard from God that a King was born in Bethlehem. That King was the entrance of God into the earth. The purpose of Jesus coming to earth was the restoration of a kingdom and a delivery of a kingdom. A kingdom is about principles, laws, and protocols. This is why the Bible is so important. It tells you what the King's protocols are. It tells you what to do. God has commissioned you to be a king like Jesus and to establish His heavenly kingdom on the earth. God made man in His image so man could have dominion over all the earth. God created Adam to dominate all the earth. He wanted Adam to be king over all His creation.

Think about it. The entire earth was Adam's kingdom. When God formed Adam from the dust of the ground, He didn't merely create another creature; He made a man in His own image and crowned him with purpose. God breathed His own life into Adam, setting him apart from every other creation. Then He gave Adam dominion and authority along with the

power to rule, subdue, and manage the earth and have dominion over it. Adam was not created to be a servant of creation,
but a steward and king over it. He was placed in the Garden of
Eden as God's representative on earth, to be a ruler under the
King of Heaven. Every animal, every seed-bearing plant, every
part of the earth's order was placed under his care. What is a
kingdom? It's the realm over which a king is absolutely sovereign. It's a territory over which the king's will is done and his
values are imparted. Adam was given part of God's creation in
which to extend God's dominion.

From the beginning, God's desire was that man would walk
in authority, wisdom, and fellowship with Him. Dominion
was not about domination, but about stewardship, about governing with love, justice, and obedience to God's command.
Adam's rule reflected the heart of his Creator. All Adam had
to do was obey God and follow all of His rules. God intended
man to rule the earth like He rules the universe. Unfortunately,
Adam failed in his calling and God has chosen you to take his
place. As a king you are called to rule in life, to bring heaven's
order to earth, and to walk as sons of the King. The same
breath of God that empowered Adam to govern creation still
empowers His people today. You are royalty. You are the child
of the King. God made you a king so you can have dominion. He wants all the benefits of heaven to come into the earth
through men who have taken on the responsibility of being a
king.

From the very beginning, God has placed a divine crown upon
the head of man. It is not a crown made of gold and jewels,

but of glory and honor. David wrote in Ps. 8:4,5, "What is man that You are mindful of him, and the son of man that You would visit him? For You have made him a little lower than the angels and have crowned him with glory and honor." This means that every man carries the mark of God's greatness. You were created not as insignificant beings drifting through life, but as divine image-bearers with purpose, value, and authority. God didn't just make you; He invested His likeness into you. His glory rests upon you as a reflection of who He is. Crowning is a sacred declaration reserved for establishing royalty and rulership. Man is crowned for royalty. This is what makes him a king. A king has divine status and there is a royal presence about him that others notice.

God established man as royalty in the earth. When God made man, he crowned him as king over all His creation. Ps. 8:6 says, "You have made him to have dominion over the works of Your hands; You have put all things under his feet." Kings have a greater capacity to do things than the common, ordinary man. Kings are made in the image of God and are given territory over which they are to have and exercise dominion over. Walk in the dignity God has given you. You are not ordinary, you are crowned with His glory and honor, created to reveal His majesty in the earth. God placed you in the world to be living mirrors of His greatness, revealing His character through justice, mercy, compassion, and excellence. Every thought, every action, every act of stewardship and creativity is an opportunity to display the glory of our Creator. Let your life shine with the confidence of one who knows who he is in

Christ: a child of the King, carrying heaven's glory wherever you go.

You were created to shine, not for self-glory but to lift the name of God, making His presence visible in every corner of the earth. As you fulfill this divine calling, you are participating in the eternal work of God, transforming the world into a reflection of His divine splendor. Every throne in history, every crown of authority, and every ruler has its true origin in the hand of the Creator. Dominion is not granted by chance, wealth, or human acclaim - it is bestowed by God, the Author of kings and kingdoms. Those who are called to lead are chosen to govern with wisdom, strength, and justice, reflecting the divine order set forth by the Almighty. A king's authority is sacred; it carries responsibility over people, nations, and the purposes of God. Just as the Creator sets the stars in their place, He appoints rulers to bring alignment, stewardship, and righteousness to the earth. The crown is not merely an ornament; it is a divine mandate to exercise dominion according to God's will.

The word "dominion" is a rulership term. When you are in charge of something or rule it, you have dominion over it. Kings are crowned for dominion and rulership by the Creator. Only God can crown you. Only God can make you a king. True kings are aware that they are in authority only to the extent they are under authority. As long as Adam was in alignment with God, he dominated the earth and everything in it. The moment he sinned, his dominion ended. When a man walks away from God, he abandons his throne, he loses his crown, and he is stripped of his kingdom. Being a king is having the right character to take on the responsibility they've been given. A king must have the ability to respond to the situation at hand. Remember, greatness is not self-made. It is God-ordained. Those who rise to leadership must first submit to the One who crowns, for true kingship begins in obedience to the Creator who reigns over all of heaven and all of earth.

You were designed and made to be a king. You function properly only when you recognize and embrace that. You're created for a kingdom, a realm of dominion that forever gives glory to God, a realm that brings divine power into the earth. Every throne in history, every crown of authority, and every ruler has its true origin in the hand of the Creator. Dominion is not granted by chance, wealth, or human acclaim - it is bestowed by God, the Author of kings and kingdoms. Those who are called to lead are chosen to govern with wisdom, strength, and justice, reflecting the divine order set forth by the Almighty. A king's authority is sacred; it carries responsibility over people, nations, and the purposes of God. Just as the Creator sets the stars in their place, He appoints rulers to bring alignment, stewardship, and righteousness to the earth. The crown is not merely an ornament; it is a divine mandate to exercise dominion according to God's will.

God's idea of a kingdom is where you go out and influence and change the world around you. You're not here to have dominion over people, you're here to have dominion over the works of God's hands.

You're here to advance God's plan and purpose for those who are in your kingdom. You take dominion over anything that interferes with those plans. Acts 1:8 says, "You shall receive power when the Holy Spirit has come upon you." Being a king and having power go together. Kings don't rule their kingdom by force or by using a sword, they rule by the power of the Holy Spirit. A king without power is merely a figurehead, but a king who understands where his power comes from walks in true dominion. Power is the ability to influence, to lead, and to establish order according to God's will. When a man recognizes that he is called to be a king under the King - Jesus Christ - he begins to rule not by pride, but by principle.

True kingship and power are inseparable - but not in the way the world defines them. The world measures power by control, wealth, and dominance, but in God's Kingdom, power flows from divine authority, character, and purpose. A king rules his life, his household, and his domain through wisdom, righteousness, and obedience to God. His power is not for self-exaltation, but for service - to uplift others, bring justice, and advance God's Kingdom on earth: Remember this: you can't be a king without power, and you can't have power without submission to the One who gives it. True power is found in alignment with divine authority. To fulfill your calling to be a king, you must have God's authority and power to do it. You are authorized by God Himself to rule your kingdom on His behalf. You have the authority to bring the kingdom of heaven into the earth and change it for the better. As a king, you are an agent of change.

You were not made to simply survive life; you were made to govern it under God's authority. You were made for dominion, for kingship. You were made to advance the kingdom of God. When a man understands his divine identity, he stops living beneath his calling. He realizes he was placed on earth to advance the Kingdom of God; to bring heaven's order into earth's chaos, to influence his world with the character of Christ, and to lead with wisdom, courage, and integrity. A true king doesn't rule for himself; he rules for the good of the kingdom and for the glory of the King who appointed him. The earth is waiting for men who know who they are to stand up as kings under the King, bringing God's presence, justice, and love into every sphere of life. Wherever you go and whatever you do, you are called to bring a part of heaven to the earth. You are called to do what Adam failed to do. You are called to have dominion over the earth and do it God's way. Rule well. Reign righteously. Represent the King.

| 4 |

"THE ORIGIN OF KINGS"

Jesus didn't come to establish a religion; He came to introduce a kingdom. He didn't come to repair religion; He came to restore kings. His purpose for coming to earth was not to patch up a broken religious system; He came to restore God's original design for mankind. From the very beginning, God said, "Let them have dominion." That was the language of kingship. Adam was given authority, territory, and the mandate to rule the earth under God's leadership. But sin robbed man of that crown, leaving him bound by guilt, fear, and the hollow rituals of religion. Religion tries to reach God through human effort. The Kingdom brings God down to man through divine relationship. Jesus came preaching about the kingdom of God, not a new denomination. He came as a King, and through His death and resurrection, He restored to us what Adam lost - authority, dominion, and fellowship with the Father.

The cross wasn't about fixing rituals; it was about restoring royalty. Through Christ, you are a son, an heir, and a king in God's Kingdom. To understand Jesus, you must understand kingship. The first and original king is God. 1 Tim. 1:17 says, "Now to the King eternal, immortal, invisible, to God who alone is wise, be honor and glory." Before there were thrones, crowns, or kingdoms on earth, there was already a King seated in majesty - God Almighty. He did not rise to power; He has always had it. He was not elected or appointed; He is eternal and self-existent. From everlasting to everlasting, He reigns. God is an eternal King, the King of kings. He is immortal. He cannot die. He is invisible, above the natural world. In other words, that which is unseen is more real than that which is seen. What is seen is temporary, what is unseen is eternal. He is the only God who is self-sustained. He is the only God and He deserves glory and honor forever.

God is not just a king among kings; He is the King of kings. Every earthly ruler, every kingdom, and every power stands under His authority. He commands the universe with a word, governs history with wisdom, and rules with righteousness and mercy. Before David sang his psalms, before Solomon built his temple, before any man wore a crown, God was already enthroned in glory. His reign has no beginning and no end. He is the First King, the Original Ruler, and the Eternal Sovereign who invites us to live under His perfect lordship. So today, let every heart proclaim, "The Lord reigns; He is clothed in majesty!" (Psalm 93:1). Our allegiance belongs not to the kingdoms of this world, kingdoms that rise and fall, whose rulers come and go, but to the King who was, and is, and is to come. Our loyalty is not bound by flags, politics, or earthly power. We serve a higher Kingdom, one that cannot be shaken.

Matt. 22:2 says, "The kingdom of heaven is like a certain king who arranged a marriage for his son." The kingdom of God is about a King who has sons. This single verse reveals the very heart of God's kingdom. It's not about religion, rituals, or rules - it's about relationship and royalty. The son of a king is a prince which means he will one day be a king also. This means the kingdom of God is about a King with kings. This is why Jesus is called the King of kings. The word "king" in both Greek and Hebrew means 'ruler.' A king is one who rules. 1 Tim. 6:15 says, "God, the blessed and only Ruler, the King of kings and Lord of lords." No person has power or authority except that which is given by God. This means that everyone who has authority is accountable to God. This includes the head of a home, the pastor of a church, the CEO of a company, the judge in a courtroom, the president of a nation.

Dan. 2:44 says, "And in the days of these kings the God of heaven will set up a kingdom which shall never be destroyed." The Bible is about a King and a family kingdom. It's ruled by a Father-King who desires to raise up sons and daughters who reflect His nature and carry His authority. You are not a mere servant invited to watch the wedding; you are family, invited to take part in the celebration of the Son's union with His people. The marriage in the Lord's parable in the gospel of Matthew represents the divine union between the Son and His bride - the Church, those who are called and chosen to share in His glory. So when we talk about the kingdom of God, we are talking about a royal household, not an institution. It's about a King, His Son, and the sons and daughters who are being prepared for a royal inheritance. In God's kingdom, everything begins and ends with the King and His Son - and those who accept the invitation to the marriage become part of the royal family forever.

Daniel continues, "And the kingdom shall not be left to other people; it shall break in pieces and consume all these kingdoms, and it shall stand forever." No earthly power can rival it. No fleeting reign can withstand it. God's Kingdom is eternal, unstoppable, and sovereign. It is a Kingdom not built by human hands but established by the King of kings Himself. Daniel is prophesying about the coming of the Messiah. Jesus came to restore kings and give them a kingdom. You can't be a king without a kingdom. You are a king, and Jesus gave you back your kingship. He then gave you a kingdom to go along with your kingship. Your kingdom is built upon the fact that Jesus is the King of kings. Pontius Pilate asked Jesus, "Are you a king then?" Jesus answered, "You say rightly that I am a king. For this cause I have come into the world" (John 18:37). Jesus was born to be a king! So were you!

Kings are legal owners of property or territory. You cannot be a king unless you have property to rule over. The property of a king is called his domain. It's the place where his authority reigns supreme, the place where he has absolute power, exercises complete control, and commands respect. It is not just land or territory; it is the embodiment of his sovereignty, the sphere where his word is law, and his vision shapes the lives of all who dwell there. A king's domain is a reflection of his strength, leadership, and the order he establishes. The Hebrew word "Adonai" means 'master; owner' and these two words mean 'lord.' A lord is the master of what he owns. A lord is not just a title; it signifies ownership, responsibility, and ultimate control over what belongs to him. Kings are masters of their domain. They are lords over the property they own. All kings must have property to dominate. They must have a domain.

Ps. 115:16 says, "The heaven, even the heavens, are the Lord's; But the earth He has given to the children of men." The sun, moon, stars, galaxies, and all celestial wonders are all under God's absolute control. Nothing in the vast universe escapes His knowledge or power. It is a testimony to the sovereignty and generosity of God that he has given the earth to mankind. This is not only an honor but also a responsibility. We are stewards of His creation, caretakers of the earth, and participants in His plan for humanity. How we manage our time, resources, relationships, and influence matters deeply to God. When we recognize God's ownership of the heavens and our stewardship of the earth, we are called to live faithfully. To honor God means to act wisely, care for His creation, and fulfill the purpose He has set before us. Why did the Lord give the earth to men? Because He wants them to be lords too. He gave men property so they can be kings and lords.

You are a king, and you are a lord. You are a lord because your Father in heaven gave you property. Every day you are to walk in obedience, stewardship, and gratitude, recognizing that every blessing, every talent, and every provision you have and enjoy comes from Him. Let your actions reflect His love, your hearts remain humble, and your life be a testimony of thankfulness for the gifts you have been entrusted with. In honoring Him through obedience and wise stewardship, you will embrace the joy and purpose He has for you. Kings own land and when they give it to someone, that person becomes a lord. All true kings are automatically lords. You can't be a king without being a lord. Why? Because lords are owners of property and, if you're a king, you must have a territory to rule over. A king without a territory is like a light without a lamp-stand. To reign effectively, you must first claim your domain, take responsibility for it, and steward it wisely.

Your authority is not defined by titles, recognition, or the ap-proval of others; it is defined by the space God has entrusted to you. How you steward that space, how you govern it with integrity, wisdom, and vision, reveals the true measure of your strength. Every decision, every action within your sphere of influence reflects the depth of your character and the faith-fulness of your leadership. True authority is exercised not in domination, but in responsible stewardship and courageous guidance, honoring both God and those under your care. Lord-ship is the key to authority. When you own something, you have authority over it. There is a specific place for a king where he is to toil, rule, and exercise authority. God made Adam and put him in the Garden of Eden. That was his place. Like He did with Adam, God will provide for you when you are in your proper place. Know also that God will cultivate your place as He cultivates you.

Kings aren't simply born, they're formed. There is a spiritual process in the formation of a king. God's leaders - His kings - are shaped, refined, and forged in the fires of preparation. They are formed, not merely born. Leadership in God's kingdom is cultivated through preparation, perseverance, and obedience. The word "formed" means 'to fashion; to shape; to devise.' It comes from the idea of cutting or framing. It means 'to be squeezed into existence.' In other words, kings are formed under pressure. Kings aren't recognized by the world first. They are formed in humility, often in quiet places, away from fame and glory. David was a shepherd, tending sheep. This work taught him responsibility, vigilance, and care - qualities of a true king. Your current position, however ordinary it may seem, is a training ground for God's purpose in your life. The shepherd's field is where the king is formed.

Kings never take the easy way out. They're strong and they run to the roar. Just as gold is refined in fire, leadership is strengthened in adversity. A king who hasn't faced hardship cannot truly rule with discernment or compassion. When kings are robbed of their pressure moments, then spiritual development is hindered. They become weak and are unable to lead properly. Men who can't handle pressure can never be kings. Don't despise the difficulties you face. They are shaping you into a leader capable of carrying God's vision. Ps. 119:71 says, "It is good for me that I have been afflicted, that I may learn your statutes." Kings learn how to govern and rule when they are afflicted and under pressure. Turning you into a king involves testing. David faced Goliath and Joseph faced slavery and imprisonment.

Trials are not punishments; they are the tools God uses to develop character, faith, and wisdom. To rule properly, a king must possess the Spirit of God.

A man is not a king without having a connection to God. A heart aligned with Him experiences purpose, peace, and joy that no earthly position can provide. Without Him, greatness feels hollow, and every achievement carries the weight of emptiness. It's this divine connection that allows a king to speak life into those under their care. A man can be tall and handsome and make lots of money but without the Spirit of God he'll never be able to properly connect with those in his kingdom. 1 Cor. 11:3 says, "The head of every man is Christ, the head of woman is man." If a man doesn't have a relationship with Christ, how can he be the head of his family? Without the Spirit of God, a king is ill-equipped to serve as head over anything. Authority without divine guidance is empty; wisdom without God's Spirit is flawed. A king who relies on his own understanding rules in weakness, but a leader empowered by God's Spirit serves with discernment, justice, and enduring strength.

In the natural, kings are known for their authority, wisdom, and strategic thinking. But in the spiritual realm, kings are defined not just by what they rule over, but by how they think. Your mind determines your throne. Your mindset determines your influence. A king needs a heavenly mindset. He has to set his mind on spiritual things. Col. 3:2 says, "Set your mind on things above, not on things on the earth."

A king who focuses only on earthly gain will never rule effectively in God's kingdom. A king must lift his thoughts above daily struggles, challenges, and distractions. Setting your mind on heavenly things doesn't mean ignoring life; it means aligning your perspective with God's perspective. A king with a heavenly mindset sees the eternal picture. He knows the end from the beginning. Daily guard your mind with scripture, prayer, and meditation. Replace fear with faith, doubt with truth, and worry with wisdom.

Your thoughts shape your destiny because transformation begins in the mind. Every decision a king makes flows from his thought life. Prov. 23:7 says, "For as he thinks in his heart, so is he." You are nothing more than what's constantly on your mind. You can locate the level of your thinking by observing your dominant behavior. If you're behaving like a king, then you're thinking like a king. A corrupted mindset produces weak decisions. A godly, heavenly mindset produces righteous dominion. 2 Cor. 10:5 (TPT) says, "We capture, like prisoners of war, every thought and insist that it bow in obedience to the Anointed One." A heavenly mindset is not automatic; it's disciplined. You must capture every thought that tries to pull you into fear, pride, or selfish ambition. Every negative, worldly, or ungodly thought must submit to the authority of Christ. When anxiety, temptation, or worldly ambition arises, immediately counter it with God's truth. Your mind is your battlefield. Your throne depends on it.

In God's kingdom, it is mandatory that a king be under divine authority. Kings must submit to the laws and principles that

God has established to govern their life. In Gen. 2:16,17, God told Adam what fruit he could eat and what fruit he couldn't eat. He was establishing authority in Adam's life. He was saying, "I'm the Lord your God! I'm the Boss over you!" He said that right after He had given Adam a job to do. Gen. 2:15 says, "God put Adam in the garden to tend it and keep it." Adam knew his purpose. He knew why he existed. He also had to understand that he was in authority only to the extent that he was under authority. Adam was given dominion over the earth, yet that authority was not absolute; it was conditional, flowing from his obedience to God. He was in authority only to the extent that he was under authority. True authority is not about independence; it is about responsibility under divine order. And when you embrace this, your influence becomes both righteous and lasting.

| 5 |

"THE CHARACTER OF A KING"

Being a king has little to do with age and everything to do with character and responsibility. You don't become a king because of the years you've lived; you become one because of the weight you're willing to carry. True kingship is about responsibility, integrity, and the courage to lead when others would rather follow. A man becomes a king the moment he decides to take responsibility for his actions, protect what's entrusted to him, and walk in wisdom. Age may crown the head with gray hair, but only character crowns the heart with honor. What is character? It's the man's willingness to do what is godly, what is courageous, and what is responsible. David was just a shepherd boy when God called him a king. He didn't have the experience, the age, or the title, but he had the heart. God saw in him a spirit of courage, humility, and obedience. That's what makes a king. You can be young in years but mighty in character.

Kingship begins the moment you accept responsibility - when you stop blaming others, stop running from challenges, and start ruling your life according to God's Word. That's when heaven calls you a king. If you are not a responsible person, you are not a king. Before David held a sword, he held a sling. Before he sat on a throne, he tended sheep. God always tests a king in private before He exalts him in public. Responsibility is the training ground for royalty. If you can't handle what's in your hand now, you won't handle what's waiting in your future. David took responsibility for his flock. He protected them from the lion and the bear. God said, "If you can be faithful over sheep, I can trust you with a nation." The same is true for us. Kingship begins when we stop making excuses. When you stop saying, "It's someone else's fault," and start saying, "The responsibility is mine," you step into your royal calling.

How well do you respond to a crisis? Goliath challenged Israel to send a man to fight him. How did the people respond? 1 Sam. 17:24 says, "And all the men of Israel, when they saw the man, fled from him and were dreadfully afraid." All the older men ran away but a teenage boy rose to the challenge. He had the character to respond to the challenge at hand and would later become the greatest king in the history of Israel. With great power comes great responsibility. The word "responsibility" can be divided into two words: response and ability. Responsibility is the ability to respond to the situation at hand. Every moment brings challenges, choices, and opportunities, and how you respond reveals your character. When the challenges of life press in around you, having a godly character gives you the strength to respond with wisdom instead of emotion, with faith instead of fear, and with purpose instead of passivity.

Kings are equipped to respond to God, to family, and to society in a functional, supportive, and effective manner. The word "respond" means 'to say or do something as a reaction to something that has been said or done.' What does a true king do? He responds to the needs of those in his kingdom. Kings who are strong bear the infirmities of the weak (Rom. 15:1). A king is forever ready to make sacrifices for the greater good. A true king does more than sit on a throne. He rules with wisdom, conquers with courage, leads with vision, protects with strength, and provides with love. His authority is not about power, but about responsibility. A king's crown is a symbol of service, his victories are for his people, and his legacy is built on faithfulness. A king's greatness isn't measured by his crown, but by his character, his courage, and his commitment to those he leads. Let it be known that the greatest slave in a kingdom is generally the king who rules over it.

A king is a reflection of God on the earth. He is to be a mirror of God, not a replacement for Him. He represents God in character and dominion. He looks like God, acts like God, and talks like God. A king who reflects God on earth must walk in righteousness, justice, mercy, and truth. These are the very attributes of God's rule (Ps. 89:14). When a king rules with righteousness, he mirrors God's holiness. When he rules with justice, he mirrors God's fairness. When he rules with mercy, he mirrors God's compassion. When he rules with truth, he mirrors God's faithfulness. His authority reveals

God's love, his power reflects God's mercy, and his decisions display God's righteousness. He is called not to serve his own agenda, but to express God's rule, God's heart, and God's nature to the people he governs. When a king rules in alignment with heaven, the earth flourishes. A king who looks like and acts like God prospers in everything he does.

A king's authority Is servanthood in disguise. Even though a king possesses authority, his rule is not about domination - it's about representing God on the earth. He stands between God and the people as a mediator of God's will. True kingship is not about being over people but for people. Consider the example Jesus left us. He is the King of kings, yet He washed His disciple's feet. He wore a crown of thorns before He wore a crown of glory. He ruled by love and not by force. A true king reflects God's nature when he uses power to lift others, not oppress them; when he uses strength to protect, not destroy. A king is rooted and grounded in God, in truth, and in love. When he strays from God's pattern, everything beneath his rule suffers. Prov. 16:12 says, "It is an abomination for kings to commit wickedness, for a throne is established by righteousness." Always remember that you are not just a man with responsibility; you are a reflection of the King of Glory.

A king is God's mouthpiece; a person God speaks through. A true king is not merely a man of power; he is a vessel through whom God's voice is heard. When God establishes a king, He doesn't just place a crown on his head; He places His word in his mouth. A king's authority flows from divine alignment, not earthly ambition. His decrees carry weight because they echo the heartbeat of heaven. He has the ability to speak fluently and provides clarity with effectiveness. Followers want leaders who hear from heaven. They want to be led by a king who has had an encounter with God. Every kingdom needs a king who listens before he leads, who seeks God's counsel before giving his own. For when a king speaks under the influence of God's Spirit, his words carry life, justice, and power that cannot be shaken. His wisdom is born in the secret place, where God whispers direction, correction, and vision. For sure, a king can be no greater than his ability to hear from God.

A king has heavenly insight. He does not act on impulse but seeks heavenly insight through prayer. He pauses, bows his heart, and lifts every decision to God, trusting that guidance flows from above. He surrounds himself with wise counsel, listening carefully to those who offer understanding. He values wisdom over popularity, discernment over haste, and knowledge over pride. In every choice, he aligns his will with God's, knowing that a kingdom guided by heavenly insight stands firm, just, and enduring. This helps him lead with vision, not just authority. He sees beyond the present moment and understands the path God has set before his people. With clarity of purpose, he illuminates the destination, showing not only where they are going, but why it matters. In his guidance, the people find direction, hope, and confidence, knowing that every step is part of a divine plan. A king who provides vision helps others walk boldly toward the future God has prepared.

A king is like an umbrella who covers those under his care. He takes the pounding, so his followers won't have to. When the storms of life rage, he stands firm, spreading his covering wide to shield his people from the rain. An umbrella doesn't stop the storm, but it keeps the storm from touching those it covers. In the same way, a godly leader can't always remove hardship, but he can stand between his people and the full force of the battle through prayer, guidance, and love. Every man called by God is meant to be such a covering. He's to be a protector, a provider, a spiritual shield for his family, his community, and his kingdom. He does warfare in the spirit. He breaks down strongholds. He casts down imaginations and every high thing that exalts itself against the knowledge of God. A king serves selflessly. He lays down his life just like Jesus laid down His life for the church. Under his care the people dwell in comfort and safety.

There is an assignment from God for which every king is called upon to fulfill. A real king is called upon to sacrifice for his kingdom. A king always puts others above himself. A sacrifice is "an act of giving up something valued for the sake of something else regarded as more important or worthy." A true king is defined not by his crown, but by his willingness to sacrifice for his kingdom. He serves with courage, wisdom, and selflessness, knowing that the strength of his reign is measured by the lives he lifts and the burdens he bears for others. True leadership is not about power; it is about giving, protecting, and standing firm, even when it costs him everything. Adam had a wife, but he had to sacrifice one of his ribs to get her. He had to give something of himself. That's sacrifice. Adam had to sacrifice for Eve in order for her to come into existence. He could only claim Eve as his wife after he sacrificed for her. Any man not willing to sacrifice for his loved ones is not fit to be a king.

All kings are commissioned by God to provide for those in their kingdom. God, in His infinite wisdom, has ordained authority and appointed leaders - kings, governors, rulers - not merely to wield power, but to serve a sacred purpose: to provide, protect, and ensure the well-being of those under their care. A king's power is meant to mirror God's love and care for His people. Just as God provides for His creation, so a king must provide for his people. David's kingship was not measured by his wealth or the battles won, but by his commitment to the welfare of Israel. Kings and rulers are instruments through whom God ensures that the basic needs of people, things such as food, shelter, safety, and justice are met and provided for. Leadership is not about luxury or indulgence; it is about service and provision. The measure of a leader's success is the flourishing of those they serve.

A king is a provider. They, therefore, have a relentless work ethic. Kings handle money wisely. They don't waste money on foolish things. A king does whatever is necessary to take care of the needs of his kingdom. 1 Tim. 5:8 says that a king who does not provide for his own kingdom is worse than an infidel. A true king does not hesitate when it comes to the needs of his kingdom. He makes difficult decisions, sacrifices his comfort, and acts with courage and wisdom to protect, provide, and ensure the prosperity of his people. A king's heart is measured not by his throne or crown, but by his willingness to do whatever is necessary to meet the needs of those under his care.

Leadership is not about ease; it is about responsibility, service, and steadfast commitment to the greater good. Rom. 13:4 reminds us that leaders are "God's servants for your good." When a king provides wisely, justly, and with a heart aligned to God, the kingdom flourishes. When they fail, the people suffer.

A godly king carries a weight far heavier than the crown on his head: the responsibility to protect those under his care. Kings are the priests of their kingdom and they're to pray and put a hedge of protection around their followers. Just as God sets boundaries around His people, a godly king must watch over his kingdom. His responsibility is to protect those who cannot defend themselves, to stand between the tyrant and the slave, the oppressor and his victim. King David often acted as protector of Israel. When enemies threatened, he did not flee; he positioned himself to shield the people. David also called on God's wisdom to guide his decisions, showing that protection begins with prayerful discernment. David confronted Goliath and protected the army of Israel from the Philistine giant. On the other hand, Adam did not protect and stand up for Eve when she was confronted by the serpent. When Eve failed to protect his wife, she got deceived and this deception led to sin.

The Bible uses the image of a hedge to describe protection. A hedge is a barrier that keeps danger out while keeping the sheep safe. Job 1:10 speaks of God setting a hedge around Job. A king mirrors this by creating systems and boundaries that safeguard his people. Spiritual hedges include prayer, accountability, wise policies, and moral guidance. A leader who prays and acts in righteousness invites God's protection over those under his care. Eph. 5:28 says, "So husbands ought to love their own wives as their own bodies." Just as a man protects his body from harm, so should he protect his wife from harm. Your wife is God's daughter, and He commissions you to protect her. Your loved ones and those in your kingdom need to feel secure in your presence. When a king fulfills his calling as protector and priest, he leaves a legacy of security, faith, and hope. The people are strengthened, communities flourish, and God's glory is reflected through righteous leadership.

All kings are called upon and appointed by God to give spiritual guidance to those in their kingdom. Wisdom says, "By me kings reign, and rulers decree justice. By me princes rule, and nobles, and all the judges of the earth" (Prov. 8:15,16). Every ruler is appointed under God's sovereignty. This means their authority is not simply personal ambition or inherited power; it carries a divine responsibility. A king must guide not only with wisdom for the nation but with moral and spiritual discernment, ensuring that the people under their care are led in ways that honor God. King Solomon asked God for wisdom, not wealth or power (1 Kings 3:7-14). His prayer demonstrates that spiritual guidance is central to righteous leadership. A king who neglects this invites chaos, corruption, and moral decline in the kingdom.

God gave His Word to Adam, and it was his responsibility to teach Eve what He said. You can't teach what you don't know. This is why you need to read and study the Bible daily.

This responsibility is too great to depend on human wisdom alone. James 1:5 reminds us, "If any of you lacks wisdom, let him ask of God, who gives to all liberally and without reproach." The Passion Translation says, "And if anyone longs to be wise, ask God for wisdom and He will give it! He won't see your lack of wisdom as an opportunity to scold you over your failures, but He will overwhelm your failures with His generous grace." Leaders must be in constant prayer, seeking God's will, consulting His Word, and surrounding themselves with counsel that reflects Godly principles. A king who relies on God can guide the nation through trials, dangers, and uncertainties. God calls all kings to be spiritual beacons, guiding their people toward righteousness and wisdom. When leaders lead spiritually, the kingdom will thrive and prosper. As a king you are to embrace your God-given call to guide, protect, and uplift those under your care and authority.

| 6 |

"BIBLICAL MASCULINITY"

Fully restored masculinity is part of God's answer to the trouble on earth. Biblical masculinity is not about power for power's sake. It is about reflecting God's image, leading with integrity, loving sacrificially, and walking in spiritual authority without pride. A true man of God is a protector, provider, and spiritual leader who exemplifies Christ in his character, decisions, and relationships. True biblical masculinity is not measured by power, wealth, or dominance; it is defined by strength under God's guidance, humility, and a heart devoted to righteousness. A godly man leads by example, protects and provides for those entrusted to him, and stands firm in his faith, even when the world challenges him. Biblical masculinity embraces responsibility, courage, and discipline, yet it is also compassionate, tender, and loving. It is a masculinity that honors God first, serving others selflessly while modeling integrity, honesty, and moral courage.

A man of God is a servant-leader: he sacrifices for the good of others, seeks wisdom from scripture, and strives to reflect

Christ in every action. True strength is found not in asserting oneself over others, but in submitting to God's authority, walking in faith, and pursuing righteousness with unwavering dedication. A masculine king is armed for battle, ready for anything, and solid through and through. Josh. 1:7 says, "Be strong and courageous." These qualities are what defines biblical masculinity. As the king goes, so goes his kingdom, his family, his church, his city, and the nation he lives in. A king who is masculine faces adversity with problem-solving strength and courage. He's a leader who won't be deterred by trouble, chaos, or calamity. A king walking hand-in-hand with God is one of the most powerful weapons to bring forth life as it was meant to be. Masculine kings are the men who rise up and go into battle for a greater good.

All kings are called to rule and reign and bring goodness to the people God has entrusted to their care. Kings were made to protect, to provide, to come through in a manner that allows others to rest. A king is not crowned to sit idly on a throne. True greatness is revealed in motion through bold decisions, unwavering courage, and the willingness to step into the arena when challenges arise. Kings are made for action, not comfort; for leadership, not passivity; for influence, not silence. Every moment presents a call to move, to fight for justice, to lead with vision, and to make a lasting impact. As a bearer of God's image, what a king brings to any situation is his masculine strength. Kings were made to face problems head on, to rise to the occasion. They are made to engage, to act, to offer a strength in love and sacrifice so that others can flourish. The kings crown may be heavy, but it is not meant to be laid aside. It is meant to guide, to act, and to conquer the impossible.

Kings are forged in the fires of battle, trained and tested for war. They endure trials, face enemies, and carry burdens so that others may live in peace. Every sacrifice they make, every challenge they overcome, is a shield for the safety and freedom of those they lead. True greatness is not measured by comfort, but by the courage to stand in the storm so that others may rest in calm. Kings were made for war so that others may experience peace through their sacrifice. Jesus said in Matt. 10:34, "Do not think that I came to bring peace on earth. I did not come to bring peace but a sword." Jesus came to put a sword in your hand, to train you to be a warrior, to be a masculine king. With a sword in your hand, you will be unafraid of conflict when it comes in the pursuit of righteousness. A sword symbolizes a man whose heart and strength are being restored to masculinity. It's for the man whose soul is rugged and tender, brave and kind, daring and playful. Just like Jesus.

True masculinity begins not with strength, power, or recognition, it begins when a man fears God. Reverence for the Lord shapes his character, governs his actions, and gives him a courage that no worldly force can match. A man who fears God honors truth, protects the weak, leads with integrity, and stands firm in the face of challenges. Fear of the Lord is the foundation of wisdom, discipline, and moral courage - the very roots of genuine manhood. It's the reverential awe of God that makes you capable of facing life's biggest challenges and coming out victorious. A man may gain the world, but without

God at the center of his life, his strength is empty. True masculinity is born when a man bows before his Creator, knowing that his greatest power flows from his obedience and devotion. The fear of the Lord is the foundation of wisdom, discipline, and moral courage, the very roots of genuine manhood.

Many men think courage is simply facing danger without fear. True courage, however, is trusting God in the face of fear. A man who fears God can confront challenges boldly - not because he is reckless, but because he knows God is his shield, his guide, and his strength. David faced Goliath not because he was a giant-slaying hero, but because he feared God and trusted Him to fight on his behalf. Masculinity grounded in fear of God is a masculinity rooted in faith, not in ego. A man who fears God is a leader in his home, in his church, and in his community. He knows he will give an account to God for how he leads. Worldly power fades, wealth disappears, and physical strength diminishes. But a man who fears God leaves a legacy. Think of biblical men like Joseph, Daniel, or Nehemiah. These were men who feared God, and through their reverence, left a mark that lasted generations.

If you want to be strong, respected, and honorable, then fear God with all that is in you. Fear God in your decisions. Fear God in your relationships. Fear God in your work. Fear God in your prayers. When you fear God, everything else falls into place. Your strength will be rooted in righteousness, your courage in faith, and your influence in godly wisdom. Prov. 8:35 says whoever finds wisdom finds life and obtains favor from the Lord. It is through wisdom that kings learn how to rule, how to be the leader God calls them to be. Respect God because He is sovereign and holy. Respect His Word, His law, His power, and His authority. Fear His displeasure, His right to chasten, and His right to judge. Failure to fear the Lord is the pathway to oblivion (Prov. 1:28-32). A masculine king walks in wisdom, knowledge, discretion, and understanding. Let your masculinity be defined not by muscle or might, but by character, courage, leadership, and lasting influence.

All of life, and this includes masculinity, is about guarding your heart. Prov. 4:23 says, "Keep your heart with all diligence, for out of it spring the issues of life." Your heart is the "control center" of your life. It's the center of your thoughts, desires, and emotions and it shapes every decision you make, every word you speak, and every action you take. To "keep your heart" means to protect it from negativity, deceit, and anything that could lead you away from God's path. It calls for you to be intentional in what you allow into your mind and soul: the thoughts you dwell on, the relationships you nurture, and the influences you embrace. When you guard your heart diligently, you cultivate wisdom, integrity, and peace. You create a life that reflects God's love and truth, because everything you produce - your words, your actions, your choices - flows from the condition of our heart. Be vigilant in nurturing your inner life, filling it with God's Word, His love, and His guidance.

Prov. 2:10,11 says, "When wisdom enters your heart, and knowledge is pleasant to your soul, discretion will preserve you; Understanding will keep you." Be careful how you think because your thoughts result in actions that have either a positive or negative effect upon your territory, upon your sphere of influence. Guard your heart from the snares of the enemy because the condition of your heart will affect everything else in your life. Everything begins in the heart. What fills your heart shapes the thoughts you dwell on, and those thoughts eventually guide your actions. Your actions, when repeated, become habits. And your habits, whether good or bad, lay the foundation of your character. Guard your heart carefully, because it's the source of everything you do (Proverbs 4:23). If your heart is filled with faith, love, and integrity, your actions will follow in that same spirit. Over time, those godly actions will form habits that define who you truly are - a person of character, molded by the heart of Christ within you.

Set a watch over your heart to keep out evil thoughts, unholy affections, and vile imaginations. Exert yourself with great earnestness, laboring to preserve your heart's vitality, vigor, and purity. At the same time, you need to watch the words you speak. Ps. 141:3 says, "Set a guard, O Lord, over my mouth; Keep watch over the door of my lips." Prov. 4:24 says, "Put away from you a deceitful mouth, and put perverse lips far from you." Your words matter far more than you may realize. Words have the power to build up or tear down, to bless or to curse, to help or to hinder. Masculinity will cause you to use your words in the most productive, powerful way and avoid bringing hurt and harm to others. Prov. 10:11 says, "The mouth of the righteous is a well of life." Let God control your speech because "the tongue of the righteous is choice silver" (Prov. 10:20). The good news is that when you let God control what you say, He can then easily control the rest of you.

Deut. 5:16 gives a command that every king should follow, "Honor your father and your mother, as the Lord your God has commanded you, that your days may be long, and that it may be well with you in the land which the Lord God is giving you." This command is not just for juveniles. This is for every man at every age for it goes far beyond simply doing what they tell you while you're under their roof. True obedience is revealed in how you live out what they taught you long after you've grown up. If your parents raised you to walk in integrity, to love God, to respect others, and to live righteously, then the greatest way to honor them is to continue in those ways. The lessons they instilled were meant to guide your steps, not just in childhood, but through every stage of your life. Listen to what your parents told you. Prov. 4:20 says, "My son, give attention to my words; Incline your ear to my sayings."

When you choose to follow through on the principles they taught you - when you treat people with kindness, tell the truth, work hard, and serve God faithfully - you are showing the world the fruit of their labor. You're saying, "I listened, I learned, and I'm still living what they taught me." The Bible says in Eph. 6:1-3, "Children, obey your parents in the Lord, for this is right. Honor your father and mother, which is the first commandment with a promise, so that it may go well with you and that you may enjoy long life on the earth." Honoring your parents isn't just about words or gestures; it's about continuing their legacy of wisdom and godliness. When you carry their values forward, you make their teaching eternal. You become living proof that what they poured into you took root and still bears fruit. So today, honor your parents not only with gratitude, but with obedience in action. Live out what they taught you and let their faith and love echo through your life.

A king also chooses his friends very wisely. They choose friends who lift them up, not the kind who pull them down. Choose friends who are honest and committed to spiritual wisdom. Choose friends who will help you "walk in the way of goodness and keep to the paths of righteousness" (Prov. 2:20). Not everyone who walks beside you is meant to walk you forward. The people you surround yourself with will either pull you closer to your purpose or pull you away from it. Choose friends who speak life into your dreams, who challenge you to grow, and who celebrate your progress instead of resenting it. True friends won't drag you down with negativity, gossip, or compromise. Instead, they'll lift you higher with encouragement, wisdom, and faith. Be around those who remind you of your worth, not those who make you question it. Remember that it's better to walk alone in the right direction than to be surrounded by people leading you the wrong way. Choose wisely for your circle of friends shape your future.

True wisdom teaches us to keep our friends within reach, but no closer. The truth is, those closest to you can cause the most harm. Paul said in 2 Tim. 4:10, "For Demas has forsaken me, having loved this present world." Relationships thrive when there is both connection and space - when love is genuine but not possessive, when care is offered without control. Closeness without boundaries can breed misunderstanding or dependency, while distance without warmth breeds isolation. True friendship requires both connection and healthy boundaries. Keep your friends close enough to share your heart, your laughter, and your journey, but not so close that you lose your sense of self. When relationships are built on mutual respect and space, they thrive. Too much distance breeds coldness; too much closeness can create dependency. Wisdom is knowing how to maintain the balance - close enough to care, but far enough to stay clear.

A shield only works if the enemy is on the other side. Be careful of the snakes in your garden. Prov. 1:10,15 says, "My son, if sinners entice you, do not consent. My son, do not walk in the way with them, keep your foot from their path." You choose your friends, don't let them choose you. True friendship requires both connection and healthy boundaries. Keep your friends close enough to share your heart, your laughter, and your journey, but not so close that you lose your sense of self. When relationships are built on mutual respect and space, they thrive. Too much distance breeds coldness; too much closeness can create dependency. Wisdom is knowing how to maintain the balance - close enough to care, but far enough to stay clear. We are called to walk with others, to love deeply, and to bear one another's burdens. But even in friendship, there must be balance. Proverbs 25:17 says, "Seldom set foot in your neighbor's house, lest he become weary of you and hate you."

Healthy friendships honor God by respecting the individuality of others while staying near enough to encourage, support, and uplift. Love does not cling - it gives. When you learn to hold your friendships with open hands, you make room for

God to remain at the center, guiding every bond in grace and truth. The people you surround yourself with shape who you become. Proverbs 13:20 says, "Walk with the wise and become wise. for a companion of fools suffers harm." When choosing friends, look for those whose hearts are set on spiritual growth. Friends who pray with you, challenge you to live with integrity, and remind you to trust God when life gets difficult. These are the relationships that strengthen your faith and draw you closer to Christ. "As iron sharpens iron, so one person sharpens another" (Prov. 27:17). Take a moment today to thank God for the friends who walk in truth and ask Him to give you wisdom to build your circle around those who pursue His righteousness.

| 7 |

"CALLED TO BE GREAT"

God calls every man to be great, and He expects you to fulfill that call. You can't be a king and not be great. If you are a Christian man, you have been chosen not only to be saved in heaven but to be great on the earth. From the moment you were born, heaven marked your life with purpose. You were not created to live small, defeated, or ordinary lives; you were created to walk in power, courage, and faith. God designed you to lead, to build, to protect, and to impact your world for His glory. Greatness in God's Kingdom isn't about fame or success; it's about obedience and faithfulness. When you answer His call, when you choose to stand strong in the face of adversity and live according to His Word, you step into the destiny He prepared for you long before you were born. You were created for substance and significance. Men slowly die on the inside when they don't know why they're here. It is God's intention for you to be great. It is not His will for you to be average.

A godly man is not called to blend in with the rest of the world; he's called to stand out. God never designed His sons to live ordinary lives. You were not called to fit in with the world; you were called to change it. When the Spirit of the living God dwells inside you ordinary ceases to be an option. From the beginning, God has called men to rise above the common, to lead with courage, to love with compassion, and to live with conviction. David wasn't ordinary when he ran toward Goliath. Daniel wasn't ordinary when he prayed in the face of persecution. Joseph wasn't ordinary when he forgave those who betrayed him. Each of them chose obedience over comfort, faith over fear, and purpose over popularity. A godly man walks in excellence because he serves an excellent God. He refuses to settle for mediocrity in his walk, his work, or his worship. He understands that being extraordinary isn't about fame or power - it's about reflecting the character of Christ in everything he does.

Greatness is defined by purpose. It is not measured by status, wealth, or the applause of men - it is measured by purpose fulfilled under the rule of God. Every man and woman was created with divine intent, a unique assignment crafted by the Creator Himself. To walk in greatness is to walk in obedience, to hear the voice of God, and to do what He has called you to do. Many men are successful but they're not great. They ignored the call on their life in order to obtain fortune and fame. Greatness is when you achieve the reason for which you were created and maximize your influence in the lives of others. Greatness is not found in climbing to the top of worldly success, but in kneeling before the King and saying, "Noy my will, but Yours be done." When you submit your life to God's authority, your purpose becomes clear, your steps are ordered, and your life begins to bear eternal fruit.

The world celebrates achievement, but heaven celebrates alignment - being in the right place, doing the right thing, for the right reason, under the right King. So, pursue not your own greatness, but God's greatness through you. For when you live in obedience to His rule, you will fulfill your divine purpose and that is what greatness is all about. You will know you are great when your children want to be around you and your wife don't want to leave you. You're great when other men respect you. You're great when you're producing something that will benefit others. Whenever God used a man in the Bible, he always called them to do something more than they thought they could do. Moses was the meekest man on the face of the earth, yet God said to him in Ex. 7:1, "I have made you as God to Pharoah." That's greatness! Big problems appear small when you're connected to the God of the universe.

When a man aligns himself under the rule of God, he steps into a life of divine order and purpose. He is no longer subject to the whims of the world or his own limited understanding. By submitting to God's authority, he positions himself for greatness, for true success is found not in self-exaltation, but in obedience to the One who sets the course of destiny. Greatness follows those who faithfully walk under His rule, for they operate under the power and wisdom of heaven. When a man aligns himself under the rule of God, he has positioned himself for greatness. God told Abraham in Gen. 12:2, "I will bless you and make your name great." He said to David, "I have made you a great name, like the name of the great men who are on the earth" (2 Sam. 7:9). In God's kingdom, greatness is granted if, and only if, you fulfill what you've been called to do. Listen to God and He will tell you what His purpose for your life is.

To discover your calling, you must first learn to listen. In the stillness of your heart, in moments of prayer and reflection, He speaks. When you tune out the noise of the world and focus on Him, clarity comes. His voice may be gentle, a whisper in your soul, or it may come through the doors He opens along your path. When you take the time to quietly listen to God, He will guide you. In His presence, the purpose He has for your life becomes clear. Trust in His voice, follow His leading, and watch how He directs your steps toward the destiny He has prepared just for you. Judges 3:31 tells how God used a farmer names Shamgar to be a judge and deliver Israel from the Philistines. He killed 600 of the enemy with an ox goad and became great because of the difference he made. The name "Shamgar" means 'the one who listens to God.' He's a farmer who's out in the field listening to God. God spoke to him, Shamgar listened to what God said, and he went out and become great.

True greatness doesn't come from chasing titles, money, or recognition. It comes when you stop trying to figure it all out on your own and let God tell you what to do. Remember, that's what the word "Lord" means. If Jesus is your Lord, then He has the right to tell you what to do. Satan wants to remove the word "Lord" but let you keep the word "God." If that happens, you'll act religious, but God is not telling you what to do. Instead of becoming great, you invite chaos, confusion, and calamity into your world. But when you listen to God's voice, follow His guidance, and step into the assignments He gives you, your life begins to shine with purpose, influence, and lasting impact. Greatness isn't self-made - it's God-directed. It comes when you stop striving to impress others, stop chasing what seems impressive to the world, and begin listening to the voice of the One who knew your purpose before you were even born.

When you allow God to tell you what to do, you step into a path that is uniquely yours. He knows your strengths, your weaknesses, your gifts, and the opportunities that only you can fulfill. Following His guidance is not always the easiest path. It often requires humility, patience, and the willingness to step aside from your own plans. But this is where greatness is born - not in self-promotion, not in comparing yourself to others, and not in the pursuit of fleeting success - but in obedience, faithfulness, and surrender to God's will. Allowing God to tell you what to do also keeps you aligned with His purpose. When you rely solely on your own understanding, you risk heading down paths that may seem right but lead to emptiness or failure. But when you seek His counsel in prayer, study His Word, and pay attention to the doors He opens and closes, you will walk in the fullness of His plan. We become instruments of His will, and in that alignment, you will become great.

Greatness starts with surrender. It doesn't come from wealth, influence, or personal talent. It comes from positioning yourself under the authority of the One who created you. God's ways are higher than yours, and His plans for your life are perfect. When you willingly submit to His guidance, instruction, and correction, you align yourself with His power and favor. Greatness in God's kingdom starts with humility - recognizing that your strength is found not in asserting control over your life, but in surrendering it to the One who knows the end from the beginning. The moment you place yourself under His authority, you are lifted above the limitations of pride, fear, and self-reliance. Follow His ways and watch Him lift you higher than you could ever go on your own. You must walk in accordance with the nature of authority, recognizing that Jesus has supreme authority over everything. True power is born in obedience to that authority and not self-will.

Jesus has supreme authority over all of reality both seen and unseen (Col. 1:16-20) so don't let the devil distract you. Align yourself and keep focused on what God wants you to do. Remember, the first step to greatness is not to demand your own way - it's to obey God's way. Let Him lead, let Him teach, and let Him mold you. True greatness is born in surrender. A king with a masculine soul draws his heroic strength from consciously submitting to a higher authority. He is a man who has given his full consent to the Lord of lords to lead him and tell him what to do. A king is a man who has crucified self-sufficiency in exchange for a reliance on God's wisdom, direction, and authority. This exchange empowers him to act in a manner that conforms to the will of God and makes a way for the impossible to become possible. True power rises not from pride, but from disciplined obedience to what is greater than himself.

God prizes your willingness to put yourself under His authority and to make Him your refuge and your strength. It is in this deliberate surrender - acknowledging a power greater than himself that a king finds courage, wisdom, and unwavering resolve. True heroism is born not in defiance, but in disciplined obedience to principles that transcend personal desire. The king who rules his own heart while honoring a higher law becomes a force of strength, protection, and inspiration for all who follow him. Being under the authority of Almighty God is the secret weapon to a powerful life. Living in alignment with kingdom authority is where the soul of a king thrives and the world is made a better place. Allow God to have the final say over everything you say and do, over the moment-by-moment realities of your life. The degree to which you live in consent to God is the degree to which you will become the kind of man to whom He can entrust His kingdom.

It's from this consent to God's authority that allows a king to flow in strength, courage, and love. Real power isn't in what you can do - it's in whose authority you live under. Submit to Almighty God, and nothing can stop you. Under God's authority, the weak become strong, and the ordinary become unstoppable. True power isn't earned - it's surrendered. Yield to Him, follow His plan, and watch ordinary moments become extraordinary victories. When you submit to His guidance, His power flows through you in ways nothing else can replicate. His authority protects, directs, and strengthens you. It turns weakness into strength, trials into triumphs, and ordinary moments into extraordinary victories. A life surrendered to God's will is unstoppable, because it is anchored in the One whose power knows no limits. To live powerfully, start by yielding completely to His authority - let His Word, His Spirit, and His plan govern every decision. That's the ultimate strategy for victory in every area of life.

Men become kings when they are willing to bring their own strength under the care and connection to the One who is greater still. The power and provision that flow out of you as a king do not originate from your own strength, wisdom, or effort - they come from your union with the Heavenly Father, when His strength becomes your strength. When you are aligned with Him, seated in His authority, and walking in obedience, His resources, favor, and power become your portion. Every decision you make, every word you speak, and every act of leadership is strengthened by His presence within you. When you yield yourself wholeheartedly to the Father, you'll be liberated from the limitation of your own will and from the tyranny of unmet desires. Consenting to God's authority enables you to not only survive the unknown but to flourish in it. It is from this submission to God that you rule with the heart of a servant and serve with the heart of a king.

True kingship is not about self-reliance; it is about being a vessel through which God's kingdom is expressed. As you remain in intimate connection with the Father, His provision flows through you, enabling you to bless others, advance His purposes, and carry out your divine assignment with authority and confidence. Remember, the throne you occupy on earth is an extension of the throne of heaven. Your union with God is the source of your influence, your strength, and your ability to lead with wisdom, courage, and grace. God doesn't call you to greatness for your own glory. He doesn't measure success by how many applaud you, how much you achieve, or how far you climb. True greatness in His eyes is not about self-promotion - it's about surrender. God wants you to be great for Him, to use your gifts, your influence, and your life to advance His Kingdom, to shine His light, and to reflect His love in a world that desperately needs it.

The life of a king is a platform for God's glory. When your greatness serves God, it has eternal impact, touching lives far beyond what you can see. Remember: your purpose is not to impress people - it's to honor Him. The life of a true king is never about personal power, prestige, or possession - it is about purpose. God raises up kings not to showcase human greatness, but to reveal His divine glory through them. A king's throne is meant to be an altar where God's will is done on earth as it is in heaven. Every victory, every decision, and every act of leadership becomes an opportunity for God to be seen, known, and exalted. When a king walks in obedience, his reign becomes a reflection of heaven's order. Justice, mercy, and righteousness flow through him like streams of living water. You become a king not to rule, but to reveal. Your platform, your influence, your story all exists for one purpose: to make God famous through your life.

Your greatness is measured by the impact you make in the lives of others, by how you lift, love, and lead them closer to God. The more you serve, the greater you become because greatness in God's kingdom is not about being above others, but beneath them, washing their feet. God wants greatness to come to you and then flow through you into the lives of others. Your usefulness is what determines your value. David served his generation. The people knew he was there because he made a difference in their lives. The Bible says he was a man after God's own heart. He wasn't perfect but he impacted his generation with all his soul and might. Like David, God has a purpose for you and it's a great one. His purpose is to maximize His divine design for you. Become great. Don't be a man who's here today and gone tomorrow. You're not here to just live and die. You're here to make a positive difference in this world. You're here to be great.

| 8 |

"ENTRUSTED WITH POWER"

Deep down, every man of God carries a desire to be powerful - not for pride or control, but because he was created in the image of a powerful God. From the beginning, God placed in man the instinct to lead, to build, to protect, and to overcome. This desire for power is not evil; it's divine when it's submitted to God's purpose. This desire is common to all men. At least it should be because that's how God designed you. Desire reveals design and design reveals destiny. The desire to lead, care for, and bring goodness to the world you live in is central to your soul. True power is not measured by how many people you can command, but by how completely you yield yourself to God's will. A man who walks in obedience carries a power greater than any earthly ruler - the power of the Holy Spirit. When a man discovers that real strength flows from surrender, he steps into his rightful place as a vessel of God's authority on earth.

Every man of God is born with the potential to be powerful but only those who humble themselves before the Lord will ever rise to it. What is power? It's the masculine surge of fierce mastery over a domain. It's the divine drive in a man to take responsibility, to bring order from chaos, and to rule with strength and wisdom. It's not domination, but direction - the disciplined force that builds, protects, and governs. True power is not wild aggression; it is controlled intensity. It is the fire that refines, the courage that stands firm, and the authority that turns potential into purpose. A man walking in his God-given power doesn't seek to overpower others - he seeks to master himself, his calling, and the territory God has entrusted to him. Power used the right way can change the world you live in. It will help you lead with courage and wisdom. Way back in Genesis, God breathed life into Adam so that he might rule and reign with power under the authority of His goodness.

The first assignment ever entrusted to mankind was to operate in God's power - to rule, to subdue, and to manifest His nature on the earth. With deep anticipation, God said to Adam, "I want you to rule with My power." He's saying the same thing to you. Dallas Willard said, "The primary work of God is finding a man to whom He can entrust His power without bringing harm to themselves and those under their care." Being entrusted with power is an invitation to become who you were meant to be. God didn't design man to operate in human strength, but in divine partnership. From Eden onward, humanity's purpose has been to represent heaven on earth - to speak with God's authority, to act with His wisdom, and to walk in His presence. You were made to bear the image of God. You're to be strong and true, to be powerful and walk in integrity. You're to partner with God to fulfill His purpose in these days in which we now live.

When God created Adam, He breathed His own life into him and gave him authority over the earth. This wasn't just a gift; it was a mission. When you step into that original design - living and moving by the Spirit - you fulfill what God intended from the start: a people operating in His power, carrying out His will, and revealing His glory. John Eldredge said, "The great problem of the earth and the great aim of the masculine journey boils down to this: when can you trust a man with power?" The answer is when a man begins to realize that life is not all about him. It's when he comes to the realization that his decisions have deep consequences in the lives of others. It's when he has the ability to maintain his integrity while under the weight of responsibility that being powerful demands. God designed you to be powerful, to be a wholehearted king. You're here to delight the heart of God through what you do with the power He gives you.

Take it upon yourself to desire more of God's favor and more of His power. Ask for more influence and more responsibility. When you ask God for more influence, you're not being selfish you're positioning yourself to make a greater impact for His Kingdom. When you ask for more responsibility, you're showing Him that you can be trusted with what He's already given you. Don't settle for where you are. God never intended for your walk with Him to be stagnant or limited. He wants to pour out more of His favor, more of His power, and more of His anointing upon your life. Desire to become the type of man with whom God is glad to entrust more and more of the care of His kingdom. You were created to be powerful and to rule. You were made to govern as a king over your kingdom. God's power doesn't run out. His favor doesn't fade. He's looking for those hungry enough to ask for more and faithful enough to handle it.

The truth is, God is always looking for vessels He can pour more into - vessels that will use His blessings to bless others. The more influence you have, the more people you can reach. The more power you carry, the more the enemy trembles. The more responsibility you take on, the more God can entrust you with heavenly assignments. As a man, you've been ordained to dominate the earth (Gen. 1:28). You're a king so act like one. Eccl. 8:4 says, "Where the word of a king is, there is power." When a king speaks, his word becomes law - it is backed by the full authority of his throne. A king's order never gets turned down. From this day forward begin to decree as kings and it shall be so in Jesus' name. Job 22:28 says, "You will also declare a thing, and it shall be established for you; So light will shine on your ways." Rise up and become all God has called you to be. You're a king so decree good things into your kingdom right now.

A king's word is powerful because of who he is. His words are not weak or empty but are alive and active because the throne gives meaning to what he says. When a king speaks, things happen. When you speak His Word by faith, that same royal power flows through you. As a king, your words carry spiritual authority when aligned with His Word. When you speak the Word of God, you're not speaking ordinary words - you're releasing royal decrees. Jesus is the King of kings, and He lives inside you. When you declare healing, the power of the King is in that word. When you declare provision, the authority of heaven moves to fulfill it. When you declare peace, storms must bow to the King's command through you. Your words, spoken in faith, have authority. They carry weight in the spiritual realm because God honors the faith of those who trust Him. Heaven always backs up what you declare by faith.

When God saved you, He didn't just rescue you from sin - He crowned you with purpose. Salvation isn't just about being forgiven; it's about being elevated. When He saved you, He made you a king, seated in authority over your life, over fear, over doubt, and over every circumstance that once held you captive. You may not look like a king or act like one, but you are one. Your day of salvation was a day of coronation. Step into the throne He has prepared for you. Walk in the confidence, the dignity, and the power of the kingdom He has given. On the day you got saved, God put you on the throne alongside Jesus Christ. You are seated in heavenly places (Eph. 2:6). This is more than a position; it is a declaration of victory, authority, and rest. From this place, you are above every fear, doubt, and limitation the world can throw at you. As a king, you are to live in the fullness of what He has already accomplished for you.

When you sit with Christ in the heavenly realms, you rise above limitations and walk in divine strength. That being so, why then do most men live like slaves? Don't be a slave when

Jesus died to make you a king. Stop living in chains when Jesus' blood set you free to rule." A king does not bow to circumstances; he rises above them. No matter the storms that rage, the obstacles that appear, or the pressure that weighs him down, he walks with authority, vision, and purpose. Kings live not by what surrounds them, but by who they are called to be. Their mindset, faith, and resilience lift them above the trials of life, enabling them to turn challenges into steppingstones and opposition into opportunity. Your circumstances do not define your throne - your character, courage, and conviction do. Just like a giant oak tree is hidden in an acorn, the potential to rule as kings is seeded in the heart of every man. Be determined to live like a king. Being a king means what you want done, gets done.

You have been given the responsibility to act like a king because you are one. Make no mistake, the path of being a king is narrow and only a few choose it. Will you be one of the chosen few? God has a divine plan for your life, and He has already prepared blessings, opportunities, and favor for you as a king in His kingdom. You are not called to live small or settle for less. Everything God has set aside for you is meant to be pursued with faith, boldness, and diligence. Go after everything God has prepared to give you as a king. Be open for a radical reconstruction of your life as God turns you into the king He wants you to be. Yes, there is more to be had, more to be grasped onto. Search your heart and engage your curiosity as you imagine the king you can become. Choose to trust God to turn you into the type of man that He can gladly entrust a part of His kingdom to, a man to whom He can give His power and authority.

You can become one of the chosen few to reach the plateau of becoming a king in God's kingdom. Yes, the climb to the top is hard and grueling but it's an adventure worth taking. The rewards of making this climb successfully will change your life forever and those you've been entrusted to rule over. God has already prepared greatness for you. Don't wait and let your destiny pass you by. Do not wait for the perfect moment or let fear hold you back. Step into the authority He has given you, walk in confidence, and claim what is rightfully yours. Your inheritance, your purpose, and your victory are already prepared for you so go after them with the heart of a king. God has already prepared greatness for you. Don't wait and let your destiny pass you by. Go after every blessing, every opportunity, every promise. Step into your authority, walk like a king, and claim what's rightfully yours. You were made for this!

Before you can rule a kingdom, you must first master the kingdom within yourself. Your power lies in your ability to take control of your emotions, your behavior, and your decisions. Conquer your mind, and your reign will be unstoppable. True leadership always begins with self-discipline, integrity, and the courage to govern your own thoughts, actions, and desires. Only then are you ready to lead others wisely and justly. The throne of a king is earned in the quiet battles within. Before your crown touches your head, let discipline and wisdom shape your heart. Kings are not born; they are forged in the crucible of self-mastery. Master yourself first, and the world will follow. True influence begins within. When you cultivate discipline, wisdom, and self-control, you become a force that naturally inspires others. Before seeking to change circumstances or lead others, master first your inner world, form powerful habits, and live with focus. The world responds to those who have conquered themselves.

Whatever you do, let your actions set the standard for others. Lead by example, because true influence comes not from words, but from the way you live. Practice what you preach. Live by the principles you want your followers to obey and practice. Be the benchmark. Let your actions inspire others to rise higher. Practice what you preach and others will follow the path you create. Excellence is contagious so set the standard for how others should perform. Live in such a way that your life becomes a guide for others. Whatever you do, let your faith, integrity, and love set the standard. Set the standard as God works through your actions. Protect your reputation at all costs. Your words, actions, and choices define you. Once lost, trust and respect are nearly impossible to regain. Guard your name like your life depends on it because it does. When your reputation is strong, your rivals will seldom challenge you. When it is weak, attacks will come from all corners. Stamp out the embers before they become a blaze.

Do not make decisions when clouded by emotion. Wait for a clearing and then act. When emotions run high - whether it's anger, fear, excitement, or pain - our judgment becomes blurred. What seems wise in the heat of the moment often looks different when the storm passes. Just as a pilot doesn't navigate through dense fog without instruments, we shouldn't steer our lives through emotional haze. Take a breath. Step back. Pray. Let time and peace bring clarity. When the fog lifts, you'll see the path more clearly and your decision will come from wisdom, not reaction. Also, be adaptable in your rule. The tides of change are increasing and will slowly erode any rigid structures that stand against it. Be fluid or risk being turned to dust. Beware of those who claim to have no interest in power for this is often a strategy to disarm you. When the time comes, they will strike without hesitation, and it will be too late to act.

An isolated kingdom is a vulnerable one. To be strong you must have alliances. A fortress can quickly become a prison when surrounded by enemies. To obtain a true ally, explain how your cause may benefit theirs. The ties of goodwill are but thin threads, whereas the ties of mutual interests are like chains of steel. To tap into the true potential of your power, focus your energies on a singular goal. Pay attention to the outcome people produce, not their intentions. Although many wish to do well, this does not guarantee favorable results. Face your struggles with boldness. Timid action is often met with strong opposition. When surrounded with disarray, be well ordered. When the emotions of others rise and fall, you remain calm and steady. When danger looms and even the bravest warriors shrink with fear, stand tall and face the opposing evil. Let your values be like shining beacons in the mists of disorder. Give your people something with which to orient themselves.

As a farmer tends to his fields so they may bear crops, cultivate the conditions necessary for people to flourish. Acting with haste weakens your control. When you rush, you surrender the advantage of clarity. Haste blurs discernment and blinds wisdom. Decisions made in panic often create more problems than they solve. True strength is not found in speed, but in steadiness - in the calm, deliberate choice that comes from a centered heart and a clear mind. Control is maintained when patience leads and purpose guides. Have faith that your ambitions will come to fruition and remain patient. Even when progress seems slow, remember that God is working behind the scenes. Every season of waiting is preparing you for the blessing to come. Stay patient, keep believing, and continue to move forward with faith believing that what you've prayed for is already in motion.

Put others first. The needs of the kingdom come before your own personal desires. In the Kingdom of God, greatness is not measured by how much we gain, but by how much we give. True discipleship means putting others before ourselves - choosing service over status, compassion over comfort, and obedience over personal ambition. Jesus Himself said, "The Son of Man came not to be served, but to serve, and to give His life as a ransom for many" (Matthew 20:28). When we put the needs of the Kingdom before our own desires, we align our hearts with His. Our calling is not to chase after what we want, but to pursue what God wants—to meet the needs of others, advance His mission, and bring glory to His name. Every act of selflessness builds the Kingdom and reflects the heart of Christ. So today, choose to serve. Choose to give. Choose to put others first because in doing so, you fulfill the very purpose for which you were created.

Beware of that which is easily gained. It's hard work that brings success. What's gained too easily is often lost just as quickly. True success is not found in shortcuts or quick rewards - it's built through hard work, perseverance, and faithfulness in the process. The path of diligence may be longer and harder, but it produces strength, character, and lasting fruit. Remember, what's worth having is worth working for. Be a symbol of transformation for your people, the answer to their prayers. Plan your affairs right through to the end. In doing so, you'll be able to counter the setbacks that will inevitably come your way. Eliminate your problems entirely lest they return with vengeance. Recognize greatness in others. Bestow blessings upon those who are worthy. People must feel cherished if they are to do their best work. Live by the principles you wish to see followed by those in your kingdom.

| 9 |

"HEART OF A WARRIOR"

Being a king is going to be a fight. Life is a continuous battle, be it internally or externally. A wise man once said, "We fight what is front of us so we might protect what is behind us." The enemy is aggressively waging war against you and those entrusted to your care. This is why every king needs to have the heart of a warrior. Every true king is not crowned for comfort but called for combat. Leadership in God's Kingdom isn't about sitting on a throne - it's about standing on the frontlines. A king without the heart of a warrior will lose what he's been entrusted to protect. Every king must be willing to fight - not with anger or pride, but with faith, courage, and conviction. He must defend truth when others bow to compromise. He must stand firm when storms rage and enemies rise. David was a king, but before that, he was a warrior. His victories in the pasture and on the battlefield prepared him for the palace. The same is true today.

God trains His kings in the fields of struggle so they can rule with strength and humility. To be a king after God's heart, you must also carry the spirit of a warrior. You must be bold in battle, steadfast in faith, and surrendered in obedience. Because in God's Kingdom, the crown is won by those who are willing to fight for what is right. You must become a warrior if you are going to become the kind of man God can trust with the leadership of His kingdom. The problem is that too many men want kingdoms without the willingness to go into battle not knowing that being passive will only increase the casualties. You must face the problem, do what needs to be done, and then move on to the next conquest. The motto of a warrior is, "Face It. Fix It. Forge Ahead." You must face the problem head-on, do what needs to be done with courage and faith, and then move on to the next conquest.

In life, you can't conquer what you refuse to confront. Problems don't disappear when ignored - they grow stronger in the shadows. Every battle you overcome builds the warrior within you. Don't get stuck staring at the obstacle - handle it, learn from it, and advance to the next victory. Peter says to be alert and of a sound mind, to be vigilant (1 Peter 5:8). He understood the dangers that come with spiritual complacency. The Christian life is not one of casual living but of constant awareness. To be alert means to stay awake spiritually, to be sensitive to the Holy Spirit, discerning of the enemy's tactics, and watchful over your heart and thoughts. To be of a sound mind means to think clearly, to remain steady, and not be swept away by emotions, fear, or distraction. The enemy seeks to catch believers off guard, but a vigilant believer cannot be easily deceived. When your mind is sober - anchored in truth and guided by faith - you recognize temptation for what it is and stand firm in the Lord's strength. Indeed, there is a war to be fought and you must arm yourself with courage, wisdom, strength, and endurance.

A warrior king knows that the evil in the world is real and there is much at stake. He has the ability to identify and react to any situation without hesitation. The enemy prowls like a roaring lion, seeking to intimidate, devour, and destroy. But the true warrior does not run from the roar—he runs toward it. Where fear would cause others to flee, faith makes him advance. Strength is not built-in comfort; courage is forged in the fire of confrontation. Every roar is an opportunity to stand firm, strike boldly, and demonstrate that the Lion of Judah fights alongside him. The roar is not a signal to retreat - it is a call to rise. It is in the fires of trials that men are forged into warriors. Every challenge you face is not a roadblock—it is a training ground. Don't turn away from the battle. Stand firm. Embrace the trial and let it shape you into the man you were called to be. Warriors are not in survival mode; they're always in conquering mode.

Is. 66:14 (MSG) says, "You'll see all this and burst with joy. You'll feel ten feet tall as it becomes apparent that God is on your side and against His enemies." When you see God moving in your life, you will burst with joy. His favor and presence will make you feel ten feet tall, because it becomes clear that God is on your side. You don't have to fear opposition or enemies for He has already taken your side. Let this truth fill your heart with confidence, courage, and celebration today. Joy comes when we recognize His power and protection working in our lives. Stand firm, rejoice boldly, and walk in the victory He has already won for you. It is during trials that men are trained to be warriors. Don't run away from a trial for you were not made for easy roads. Trials aren't walls, they're steppingstones. Embrace them! Don't flee the storm; let it strengthen your faith. Every trial is a training ground for your breakthrough. Run toward your challenge, not away from it. Trials refine, not define. Embrace the process!

How do you become a warrior? Francis of Assisi said, "Start by doing what's necessary; then do what's possible; and suddenly you are doing the impossible." Every great achievement begins with a single, essential step. Focus on the basics first, tackle what you can do today, and watch how your consistent effort opens the door to what once seemed impossible. Progress is a journey. One necessary action at a time leads to extraordinary results. A true warrior king is not defined by the strength of his sword or the fierceness of his battle cry, but by the depth of God's power flowing in and through him. When he surrenders his will to the Almighty, he becomes more than a man—he becomes a vessel of divine authority, wisdom, and courage. God's power equips him to face the impossible, to lead with righteousness, and to bring victory where defeat once stood.

The warrior king does not rely on his own might, but moves boldly, knowing that the same power that parted seas, toppled giants, and raised the dead now flows through him. Warriors are not self-sufficient. They know they were made by God, made for God, and made to need God. There is no stronger king than the one whose heart is fully rooted in, established in, and united with the living God. 2 Cor. 16:9 says, "For the eyes of the Lord run to and from throughout the whole earth, to show Himself strong on behalf of those whose heart is loyal to Him." Say to God, "Here I am, Lord. Look no further." He is the vine; you are the branch. Your warrior strength comes from your union with Him. The enemy knows what you're capable of. He fears what you will become in God's kingdom. Don't be the only one who underestimates your potential as a king. Let the world see that when God is at work in a man, no weapon formed against him can prevail, and every battle becomes a testament to His glory.

To be a warrior, you must know you are the apple of God's eye (Ps. 17:8). It's knowing who you are in Christ that gives you the courage to relentlessly face the enemy without fear. Your identity in Him is your greatest weapon and is what allows you to stand boldly and relentlessly against the enemy. Courage doesn't come from strength but from knowing you are a child of the King. In Christ, fear loses its power and boldness becomes your armor. When you know you are in Him, no enemy can shake your courage. God is saying to you, "Son, you are the delight of My heart. You have what it takes. I am with you. Let's fight this battle together." Having confidence that God is on your side gives you the courage to follow through. Courage is not the absence of fear. It's the refusal to allow that fear to stop you from being the best version of yourself. A courageous man goes forward no matter what's in front of him so rise up and be a warrior in God's kingdom, an unstoppable force of good in a broken world.

God's divine design for every man is to be a warrior king in His kingdom whose purpose is to bring his kingdom under the rule and reign of God's kingdom. Lives and families fall apart when you settle for anything less. Submit your will to God's will. Let Him have His way over everything you do and over every decision you make. Declare His goodness over that portion of His kingdom entrusted to your care. All warriors are enforcers. They are resilient and able to withstand or recover quickly from difficult situations. Warriors know that the kingdom of God operates on power and authority. They move with relentless determination, unwavering commitment, and quiet humility. They do not seek glory for themselves but pursue the mission with a steadfast heart that is undaunted by obstacles, driven by purpose, and grounded in discipline. True strength is measured not by power alone, but by consistency, focus, and the humility to serve a cause greater than oneself.

A warrior king is not defined by his strength alone, but by the authority God has placed in him. He stands fearless, equipped with divine wisdom, and exercises his spiritual authority to advance God's kingdom on the earth. Every step he takes, every word he speaks, carries the power of heaven. He confronts darkness, breaks strongholds, and enforces righteousness - not by human might, but by the Spirit of God working through him. A warrior king knows that his victory is certain when he aligns with God's will, for he rules with courage, faith, and the unshakable authority of the Almighty. Jesus disarmed the power of the enemy (Col. 2:15) and warriors walk in the authority of Jesus. They do not fight in our own strength but walk in the authority of Jesus, carrying His victory into every battle, speaking life over situations, and standing firm against fear, doubt, and oppression. When they fight in His name, the enemy has no power over them for their authority is given by Christ Himself.

Paul tells you what to do as a warrior king in God's kingdom. 1 Cor. 16:13,14 says, "Be watchful, stand firm in the faith, act like men, be strong. Let everything you do be done in love." A king who is a warrior is a watchful man. He is aware of what's going on around him. He's sober-minded, on guard at all times. He is careful how he lives his life and how he leads. He watches where his feet take him. He ponders his every move. He watches where he places his affections. He watches what he exposes his eyes and his ears and his thoughts to. He is a man of self-control. He is self-disciplined and has the ability to pursue what is right despite temptations to abandon it. In the Garden of Gethsemane, Jesus gave the command to the disciples to "watch and pray lest you enter into temptation" (Matt. 26:41). A king is a watchful man and a praying man. 1 Peter 4:7 says, "But the end of all things is at hand; therefore, be serious and watchful in your prayers."

A king stands and he stands firm in the faith. A king does not waver. He digs his heels in, knowing the promises of God are true. Through trials, storms, and opposition, his confidence is anchored not in his own strength, but in the unshakable promises of God. He moves with authority, guided by wisdom, and rooted in righteousness. A true king knows that victory begins with steadfast faith, and that no matter what comes, he will stand undaunted, unshaken, and unwavering. When you root yourself in truth, identity, and calling, nothing can shake you. The world may try to pull you in a hundred directions, but your foundation will hold. Your belief, your self-worth, and your mission are non-negotiable. Stand firm. Step forward with confidence. And let your life be a testimony of unwavering commitment to what truly matters. Life will challenge you. Opinions will clash. Doors may close, and storms will rise. But when you root yourself in truth, identity, and calling, nothing can shake you.

In the world you will have tribulation (John 16:33) but your faith is founded on the rock of your salvation, Jesus Christ (Ps. 62:6). Stand up and embrace your God-given identity. You are a king! Stand firm in that reality. You were made in the image of Christ. This means you are royalty. He's a King and you are too. Be a divine light in your home, your church, and your community. Make an impact in the world you live in. Stand firm and take an active role in the lives of those around you. Be the king God called you to be. You are a king so act accordingly. Stand up, stand firm, and stand strong. God calls all men to be tough. With a voice full of authority and love He's pointing His finger at you, saying, "Wake up! Be a man!" Don't be conformed to the culture of this day where men are soft and weak. The world will tell you to get in touch with your feminine side. There is nothing more pathetic than that. Don't be a sissy! Stand up and act like a man!

God doesn't call the weak to greatness. He calls ordinary men to become extraordinary through toughness, perseverance, and unwavering faith. Answer His call. Rise up. Be the man He created you to be. Stand strong. Face life with courage. Lead with faith. Your time to rise is now. Men are masculine, not feminine, so be a man who has uncompromising courage. Be brave and be strong. God designed men to lead, protect, and stand firm. Masculinity is not weakness - it is strength tempered with courage. A man of God faces challenges without compromise, stands for truth without fear, and moves forward when others hesitate. Be brave. Be strong. Be a man who lives with uncompromising courage, who stands tall in the face of adversity, and whose character cannot be shaken. True masculinity is bold, resilient, and anchored in faith. Be a man of courage and stand tall when storms rage. Let your character be unshakable, your convictions unwavering.

Having courage in the face of every temptation and danger is the trademark of every king. Be like Caleb who said in Num. 13:30, "Let us go up at once and take the land. For we are well able to take it in battle." Be the type of king where anything is possible. If God be for you, who can be against you? Grab hold of the vision of God and possess it as your own. Be the king God called you to be, a man of uncompromising courage. Stand tall in the face of adversity, refusing to bend to fear, pressure, or temptation. A man of true character does not seek the applause of others, nor does he yield to fleeting comforts. His integrity is unshakable, his convictions unwavering, and his actions consistently reflect the principles he holds sacred. Such a man knows that courage is not the absence of fear, but the mastery of it. He rises when others fall, speaks truth when silence is easier, and walks faithfully on the path of righteousness, no matter how narrow or difficult.

Let your life be a testament to strength, honor, and unwavering resolve, showing the world that a man of courage stands firm, regardless of the storms he faces. For sure, a king is a strong man, a man of integrity, a man of character, a man of the Spirit. Kings are to be strong because they have a work to do. They have an assignment from on high. Dan. 11:32 says, "The people who know their God shall be strong and carry out great exploits." A king does great things in his life, and he needs the strength of God to do them. Ps. 121:1,2 says, "I will lift up my eyes to the hills. From whence comes my help? My help comes from the Lord." A king is strengthened by the Word of God. He is strong in the Lord and in the power of His might (Eph. 6:10). Ps. 18:2 says, "The Lord is my rock and my fortress and my deliverer; My God, my strength, in whom I will trust." A king is a man whose God is his strength. Ps. 24:8 says, "Who is this King of glory? The Lord strong and mighty, the Lord mighty in battle."

| 10 |

"MENTALITY OF A LION"

In Rev. 5:5 Jesus is called "the Lion of the tribe of Judah." The lion is the king of the jungle and is a great source of encouragement to all who want to be leaders and kings. If Jesus identified Himself as a Lion, then that says something about the kind of spirit He wants His followers to walk in. He didn't call Himself a lamb in Revelation, He revealed Himself as a lion. And if the Lion of the tribe of Judah lives inside of you, then you, too, must learn to roar with the same boldness, the same courage, and the same authority. You were not created to live in fear or hesitation. The same boldness that roars through Christ now dwells in you through the Holy Spirit. When the world tries to silence your faith, remember that lions do not whisper. When trials come to intimidate you, remember that lions do not retreat. So lift your head, stand firm, and walk in the authority of your King. Let your faith roar in the face of doubt. Let your courage echo through every battle.

To rule your kingdom like a lion, you need to know the nature and mentality of this powerful animal. The lion is king not because it's the biggest or the fastest animal in the jungle. It's not because he has any great physical advantage over other animals. It's the mentality of the lion that makes him strong, that makes him the king of the jungle. The lion has what is called "the spirit of leadership." A leader has an attitude that makes him different from followers. A lion is in complete control of his life. A lion is not told by others what to do or where to go. Lions don't ask for permission to roar. They don't apologize for their strength. Wherever a lion stands, authority is established. The lion goes about his business fearlessly and with extreme confidence. The lion is not timid, silent, or passive. It rules with authority, confidence, and strength. You carry that same authority. Luke 10:19 says, "Behold, I give unto you power to tread on serpents and scorpions, and over all the power of the enemy,"

If Jesus is the Lion, then His roar should be heard through you! When you pray, pray with authority because the same power that conquered the grave now lives in you. When you speak God's Word, speak it like a lion who knows it cannot be ignored. The lion is king of the jungle because of one word. Attitude. The lion has a different attitude that makes every other animal afraid of him. For example, when a lion sees an elephant, one thing comes to his mind. Lunch! He then acts the way he thinks. He attacks the elephant. On the other hand, the elephant is bigger and stronger and more powerful than the lion. Yet when he sees the lion, he runs away because he thinks he's going to be eaten. His size and power are a victim to the way he thinks. The lion is king because of what he believes about himself. An army of sheep led by a lion will always defeat an army of lions led by a sheep. Why is this true? Because the attitude of a leader can transform cowards into violent warriors.

The lion reveals courage under pressure. It doesn't back down from a fight. They don't flee when danger comes - they face it head-on. And so did Jesus. In the Garden of Gethsemane, when soldiers came to arrest Him, He didn't run. He stepped forward and said, "I am He." That's the roar of the Lion! God is calling His people to rise up with that same courage and face every battle, every trial, and every test with the heart of a lion. Because greater is He that is in you than he that is in the world. A lion cub doesn't have to be taught how to roar because it's in its nature. Likewise, boldness is in your spiritual DNA. You are a child of the Lion of Judah! Proverbs 28:1 says, "The righteous are bold as a lion." That means you were born to walk in confidence, not fear. You were created to take dominion, not live-in defeat. You are called to reflect the image of the King of kings, not just in words, but in character and courage.

If Jesus identified Himself with a Lion, then you must do the same. Stop living like a sheep when you've been called to roar like a lion. Stop bowing to fear when the King of the Jungle lives inside of you. Let your life be a roar that shakes hell. Let your faith be a roar that drives out doubt. Let your worship be a roar that reminds every demon that the Lion of Judah still reigns! Lift up your voice and stand tall in your authority. The Lion of Judah lives in you. It's time to roar! Inside of you lies the same attitude and potential as the lion who is the king of his domain. The lion knows who he is. He walks with confidence, acts with authority, and rules his territory with courage. That same spirit of boldness, dominion, and confidence has been placed inside of you by God. You were never meant to live in fear or shrink back from challenges. You were created to rise, to lead, to stand tall in the face of adversity. Lift your head up high. Straighten your back. Remember who lives inside you.

The Lion of Judah has given you His nature and this is why kings don't bow to circumstances; they make circumstances bow to them. You need the same attitude as a lion because it has been given the same attitude God identifies with. Like the lion, you were designed to walk with a quiet strength that commands respect and to carry the heart of a king who knows his purpose. The lion is not taller than the giraffe, not bigger than the elephant, not heavier than the hippo, not faster than the cheetah, not smarter than the hyena, and not wiser than the serpent. And yet the lion is king. When he shows up, all these other animals run away. The lion is king because of what he believes about himself and what he believes about the elephant and the giraffe. His attitude is different than theirs. He believes they are lunch and that he can eat them. The difference between a leader and follower is attitude. Leaders think differently than followers.

Attitude changes everything. It produces certain behavior that will stretch you beyond your limitations. Attitude is a product of belief. It comes from what you believe. Your life is what you think it should be. If you don't like who you are, change how you think. You need the same attitude as a lion because that's the same spirit God wants in you. The lion's boldness, confidence, and dominance are reflections of divine authority. God identifies with the boldness of a lion, and He wants you to do the same. He expects you to rise up with courage, to see challenges not as threats but as opportunities to conquer through faith. So don't think small, don't run from fear, and don't let obstacles intimidate you. You've been given the same attitude as the Lion of Judah, Jesus Christ Himself. Walk in that same authority. God wants you to be fearless, confident, and unshaken. The Lion of Judah lives in you, so stand tall and roar with faith.

No amount of training can be a substitute for having the right attitude. You can teach skills, drill routines, and build experience but attitude is the heart that drives everything else. Training sharpens ability, but attitude determines direction. A person with the right mindset will find a way to grow, to adapt, and to overcome. A person with a poor attitude will find an excuse, no matter how much they've been trained. Talent may open a door, and training may prepare you to walk through it, but attitude keeps you standing when the storm hits. In every area of life - whether in ministry, leadership, or daily faith - the right attitude is what turns potential into purpose. Potential is what God places in you, but attitude is what brings it out of you. You can have all the talent, gifting, and opportunity in the world, but without the right heart posture - humility, faith, perseverance, and gratitude - potential will remain dormant.

It's the right attitude that keeps you steady when things get hard, hopeful when doors close, and teachable when correction comes. Your attitude determines how you handle the waiting, how you respond to challenges, and how you treat others on the journey. Potential is the seed. Attitude is the soil. Purpose is the harvest. When your attitude aligns with God's will, He takes the potential inside you and transforms it into divine purpose that impacts lives and glorifies His name. So if you're not yet a king, then change who you think you are. Get the mentality of a lion. Your identity determines your destiny. Stop thinking like a servant when God created you to reign. Get the mentality of a lion and be bold, fearless, and unshaken by opposition. So lift your head, square your shoulders, and walk like royalty. You were born to lead, to conquer, and to represent the King of kings. Think like a king. Move like a lion. Live like a child of God. When you do that, a great roar will arise in your heart, the roar of freedom.

In the jungle, the roar of a lion can be heard up to five miles away. That roar is a declaration of dominance, presence, and power. In the same way, when a man of God finds his roar of faith, heaven and hell both take notice. Your roar carries farther than you think so let it be heard. Of all the cats that roar - the lion, tiger, leopard, jaguar - the lion roars the most often and the longest and the loudest. When a lion roars, he means business His roar is not for show, it's a declaration of authority, a warning to intruders, and a signal to the entire jungle that he's in control. Likewise, when a man of God opens his mouth with the boldness of faith, heaven listens and hell trembles. A lion doesn't roar to prove who he is; he roars because he knows who he is. When you know the authority you carry in Christ, you don't whisper your faith, you roar it with confidence, conviction, and purpose. Be a king who stands boldly, speaks boldly, and live body for you are seated in heavenly places.

Nothing compares to the roar of a lion. A lion's roar has such force that it can lift the dust off the ground and create a large whirling circle of dirt in front of him. The roar has been known to cause the metal frames of vehicles to vibrate. In the natural world, a lion's roar commands attention. It shakes the earth, strikes fear in the hearts of its prey, and announces the presence of a king. But in the spiritual realm, there is a roar far greater than any sound this world can produce - the roar of God. Nothing compares to the roar of the Lion of Judah. His roar is not just noise; it is power, authority, and the call to victory. When He roars, strongholds tremble, chains are broken, and the timid find courage. His roar declares your purpose, your destiny, and your inheritance. The enemy may whisper, the storms may rage, but the roar of the Lion of Judah rises above it all. It reminds you that you are not alone, that His power is unmatched, and that you are part of a kingdom that cannot be shaken.

So when you feel weak, afraid, or overwhelmed, remember this: nothing in heaven or on earth compares to the roar of the Lion. Let His roar awakens the boldness within you, inspire your faith, and propel you into the victories He has already prepared for you. Be strong. Be courageous. Stand firm. For the Lion has roared, and your victory is assured. A lion roars for several reasons. He roars to warn off intruders, thus fulfilling his role as protector. He roars to startle prey as he gets ready to take them down, thus fulfilling his role as a provider. He roars to reunite scattered members of his domain, thus fulfilling his role as a leader. He roars to attract a female lion, thus fulfilling his role as a partner. But most of all, a lion roars to declare dominion. When a lion is in his domain, he will roar multiple times over the course of several hours. He is communicating to all other animals, "This is my territory! This is my domain!" This roar is a reassuring sound of security to the other lions under his care.

When a lion roars, he is declaring that he has authority and is responsible for what goes on in his territory. He roars to express strength, or to call out in the night. But every roar carries a message: "I am here, and I am not afraid." Spiritually, the roar of a lion mirrors the voice of God's people in a world that tries to silence faith. When a believer speaks with the authority of faith, hell trembles and darkness loses ground. A lion roars to lets every creature know that the king is awake and watching. He declares, "The Lord is with me!" His roar marks boundaries that no enemy can cross. It builds walls of faith around those under his care. A lion doesn't whisper when it's time to act; it roars. There are moments when silent faith must become bold proclamation. Your roar is your voice of faith, your praise, your declaration of God's Word. The enemy thrives on silence, but he fears a man who knows how to lift his voice in victory.

The lion stands as a timeless symbol of fearless courage. It does not back down when challenged, nor does it shrink away when surrounded by opposition. A lion has fearless courage. It will never surrender. The lion will never lie down and die, not even if surrounded by ten hyenas. Its roar declares strength, confidence, and dominion - not arrogance but assurance of identity. The lion knows who it is. In the same way, the believer in Christ is called to walk in that same kind of holy boldness. You are not to retreat in the face of trials, fear, or spiritual warfare. When God placed His Spirit within you, He gave you the heart of a lion, a heart that is unwavering, fearless, and unbreakable. The fight is never over until it is over. Lions stand up for what they believe in. They don't give up, they don't give in. When the storms of life rise and the enemy presses in, the man of God must stand firm in faith, knowing the battle belongs to the Lord. Fear has no authority where faith abides.

Let the Spirit of the Lion of Judah rise within you. Refuse to surrender to fear, doubt, or discouragement. Be fearless in going after what you really want in your life. Keep fighting. No retreat, no surrender. Be fearless in going after what God placed in your heart. Fear says, "You can't." Lions say, "Watch me. If God be for me, who can be against me?" Keep fighting for your purpose. Keep believing when it's hard. You weren't created to back down - you were created to conquer. Stand firm. Push forward. With God on your side, retreat is not an option. The enemy wants you to surrender your calling before you see the victory. But this is your time to stand firm, to plant your feet in faith and say, "No retreat, no surrender." The lion is certain. It never second guesses. There is nothing half-hearted about the lion. When he goes in, he goes in one hundred percent. Live with the certainty of the lion. Go after what you want with the same ruthless certainty of a lion as it hunts its prey.

The lion has freedom because the lion demands freedom. The lion does not bow to chains. Deep within him burns the cry of freedom - a holy defiance against anything that would confine his purpose. He was not created to live in cages but to rule the wild with strength, courage, and honor. When he fights, he does not fight merely to survive; he fights to remain free. His very nature declares, "I was born to live unbound." Fight for your freedom and the freedom of others. Break the chains of bondage that hold you back. True freedom always costs something. The lion will die before he surrenders his liberty, and the believer must carry that same resolve. Jesus, the Lion of Judah, fought for your freedom with His very life. Gal. 5:1 says, "It is for freedom that Christ has set us free." Christ has set you free, and the roar of that freedom echoes in your soul. The lion in you rises against the chains of darkness, because freedom is not just a right, it is a divine calling.

Lions sleep around twenty hours a day and yet they never go hungry. They get up and get the job done. They earn their rest. They earn their success. They earn their freedom. It doesn't matter how long you work. What matters is how good that work is. It doesn't matter how many hours you work. It only matters how much value you have created. In life, if you provide more value to others than anyone else, you will be rewarded well and often. For sure, there are great rewards for competence, for having the ability, knowledge, and skill to do something successfully. Having a roar alone isn't enough. Power without discipline is chaos. Passion without preparation is weakness. To truly represent the King, you must roar like a lion and turn yourself into a competent machine. You must be sharp, efficient, reliable, and ready for every good work. Work on what matters in your life with laser focus and ruthless determination. Have a burning desire to do everything to the very best of your ability.

When you combine the heart of a lion with the discipline of a soldier, you become unstoppable. The Holy Spirit refines your strength, directs your roar, and turns your passion into precision. With a lion mentality, you will never be defeated. You will not be pulled away from your purpose. You will not be distracted from your goals. You will not be dethroned and never be destroyed. You will wake up with purpose. You're alert and ready and focused. What you want, you go after. Whatever you go after, you obtain. If it matters to you, you will get it. You will have it. You will become who and what you want to become. The devil and nobody else can defeat you. You can only be defeated if you quit, and a lion never quits. So rise up. Roar in faith. Let your excellence reflect your devotion. Become so spiritually competent, so focused, so strong in character that the enemy trembles when he hears you move.

| 11 |

"TRUE LEADERSHIP"

All kings are called to be leaders. God, in His infinite wisdom, establishes leaders over nations, communities, and even within our own lives. The crown a king wears is not merely a symbol of honor, wealth, or status - it is a sacred responsibility. Every king, whether reigning over a nation or guiding the people in his household, is called to lead with wisdom, justice, and humility. True leadership is not about power for personal gain, but about service for the good of others. God calls kings to be shepherds to their people, guiding them through storms, making decisions that honor righteousness, and protecting those entrusted to their care. The anointing of a king is also an anointing of accountability - to rule justly, to walk in integrity, and to seek divine counsel in every decision. True leadership is not a method or a technique. True leadership is an attitude. You can't be a king if you don't have the mentality of a king. When you change your attitude, you'll change your altitude.

Every man in God's kingdom is called to a form of kingship. They are called to take dominion over their lives, their decisions, and the spheres God has entrusted to them. Take charge of your life! Stop thinking like everybody else! It's your belief system that regulates your behavior. Inside of you is great potential. Just understand that your potential is a slave to what you believe. An elephant has great power, but his belief system causes him to fear the lion. Leadership begins in the heart. It begins with courage, discipline, and the willingness to put others before self. God does not call the perfect; He calls the willing. He equips those He calls to rise to their destiny as leaders, rulers, and shepherds of their spheres of influence. Yes, a crown is heavy, but it is meant to elevate those who lead with faith, love, and humility. Every king is called to be a leader, and every leader is called to serve the people God has placed in their care.

Just as a tiny acorn holds within it the potential to grow into a mighty oak, so too does every man carry within him the capacity to lead, to influence, and to rise to greatness. The strength is already inside of each of them, it simply needs the right conditions: faith, patience, and perseverance. An acorn doesn't become a tree overnight. It faces seasons of rain, storms, and darkness underground, yet with time, it breaks through the soil and stretches toward the sunlight. Likewise, a man's journey to leadership is forged through challenges, discipline, and the courage to grow beyond comfort. God has planted greatness inside you. You may feel small, unsure, or unprepared, but within you lies the seed of influence, wisdom, and authority. Nurture it with prayer, purpose, and persistence, and you will rise—strong, steadfast, and ready to lead others into their own season of growth. The oak does not question its size when it is an acorn. It simply grows. And so must you.

True leadership cannot be taught. It must be discovered. Discover that you are important to the world, to the human race. You were born to do something great, and you must believe that to be a king. God is taking you somewhere. You have a destination, a destiny that God has ordained for you and offers to you. You are not just here to take up space, to water the lawn and watch television. You are here for more than that. You are here to rule, and to rule well. A king is here, not merely to occupy a throne, but to rule with purpose, wisdom, and justice. His authority is not a privilege; it is a responsibility. Every decision, every word, every action shapes the kingdom entrusted to him. True kingship is measured not by power over others, but by the care, guidance, and protection he provides. To rule well is to walk humbly, listen carefully, and act decisively, always seeking what is good, righteous, and lasting.

A king who rules with integrity inspires loyalty. A king who rules with love fosters unity. And a king who rules with faith honors the divine hand that placed him in leadership. Always remember that a throne is not just a seat; it is a calling. As a king you are called to rule well, to lead with courage, to serve with humility, and to leave a legacy that blesses generations. You have authority and God expects you to use it. As a king it is your responsibility to reach into heaven and bring God's authority to the earth. When a man becomes a king, authority is delegated to him from on high. When a man becomes a king, he does not earn his authority by his own strength, wisdom, or ambition alone. True authority is not self-generated - it is delegated from on high. God, the ultimate King, places the crown on the head of those He chooses and entrusts them with dominion over people, resources, and responsibilities. That authority allows him to act on behalf of God.

A king's power carries both honor and burden. The authority he wields is sacred, not merely political or social. It is a trust from God, a stewardship to lead with righteousness, justice, and humility. Every decision, every decree, every act of leadership must reflect the heart of the One who granted it. The moment a man recognizes that his authority comes from God, he shifts from ruling for himself to ruling for the greater good, guided by divine wisdom. His leadership becomes an instrument through which God's purposes are fulfilled, and his people are lifted. A king's leadership is more than a position of authority; it is a sacred instrument through which God's purposes are manifested on earth. The throne is not merely a seat of power; it is a platform for God's will to move among His people. Remember, a crown may sit upon your head, but the hand that placed it there is from above. Honor the source of your authority, and your reign will bring peace, justice, and blessing.

When a leader walks in humility, wisdom, and integrity, every decision, every decree, and every act of justice becomes a channel of divine intention. God equips leaders with discernment, courage, and vision, not for personal glory, but so that their leadership can align with His higher plan. Just as a skilled musician uses an instrument to produce harmony, a king's leadership, when surrendered to God, resonates with righteousness, bringing order, peace, and blessing to a nation. The heart of a true king recognizes that authority is stewardship. Every action guided by God becomes a thread in the tapestry of His eternal purposes, shaping the destiny of individuals and nations alike. Leadership, therefore, is not just about ruling; it is about being a vessel through which God's plan unfolds, touching lives and advancing His kingdom. The calling of a king is to lead not by ambition or fear, but by faith, knowing that in God's hands, his reign can become an instrument of His perfect will.

Every king has a divine place - a position, a calling, a sphere - where God has placed him. It is not merely a matter of ambition, timing, or human strategy. The Lord ordains the moments, the mountains, and the responsibilities in which His chosen will stand. It's now time for the men of God to roar and establish divine territory, a place where the devil can't invade. It's yours if you'll take it, if you'll take on the responsibility that goes with it. To occupy your divine place, you must first recognize that it is God who establishes you. Psalm 75:6-7 reminds us, "For promotion comes neither from the east, nor from the west, nor from the south. But God is the judge. He puts down one and exalts another." Your seat of influence is not earned but entrusted by the Creator. Being in your divine place requires wisdom, humility, and steadfast faith. A king in his place does not rule by ego but by obedience to God. Every decision, every action, every word becomes a reflection of the King's alignment with His Maker.

So, whether your place is visible to the world or hidden from the eyes of men, know this: God has set you where you are for a reason. Stand firm. Walk in integrity. Fulfill the purpose He has placed before you, for when a king occupies his God-ordained place, heaven's authority flows through him, and his influence transforms the world around him. To express your authority within your domain, you must roar. This is not an option! You must protect, provide, lead, and partner well in the area of your influence. Those under your care need to hear the reassuring strength of your roar. You must declare your dominion by responsibly exercising your rule over it. A true king in his sphere of influence understands that leadership is not about title - it's about responsibility. He must protect those entrusted to his care, standing firm against threats and guiding them through challenges. He must provide, ensuring that the needs of his people or team are met with wisdom, resourcefulness, and integrity.

He must lead with vision, courage, and humility, inspiring others to follow not out of fear, but out of respect and trust. And he must partner well, recognizing that collaboration and unity strengthen his kingdom far more than isolation ever could. A king's greatness is measured not by what he possesses, but by how well he nurtures, safeguards, and empowers those within his influence. Lead with honor, serve with love, and rule with wisdom. Your destiny is before you, shining like a path lit by God's own hand. But you cannot walk into it while carrying the weight of yesterday. Every regret, every hurt, every mistake is a chain that binds you to the past. To move forward, you must release it all. Trust that God's grace covers yesterday's failures, His love heals yesterday's wounds, and His wisdom guides today's steps. Step boldly into the future He has prepared for you. Do not look back. Do not linger in what was. The life you were meant to live is waiting on the other side of yesterday.

Josh. 1:2 says, "Moses My servant is dead; now therefore arise, cross this Jordan." Moses was great. Moses was important. But Moses was yesterday. Joshua could not go to his tomorrow until his yesterday died. Don't allow regret, sin, or even success keep you tethered to yesterday. If the devil can keep you chained to yesterday, he can stop you from reaching your tomorrow. On your car, your windshield is bigger than your rear-view mirror because where you're going is much bigger than where you came from. Yesterday will destroy your future whether it's good, bad, or ugly. Forget about yesterday. Lam. 3:22,23 says God's mercies and His compassions "are new every morning." Yesterday is a chapter already written. It holds lessons, victories, and even regrets but it is not your home. Learn from it, grow from it, and let it shape you, but do not let it define you. Take a moment to honor yesterday, to thank it for its lessons, and then lay it to rest.

Hold no grudges against yourself for what was and release the weight of what cannot be changed. Just as a funeral marks the end of a life and the beginning of remembrance, let yesterday die so that today can live fully. Walk forward with gratitude, hope, and faith. Embrace the new day as a gift, unburdened by what was, ready for what God has prepared for you. Yesterday may have taught you but today calls you to live. Life is too precious to live in the shadows of the past. Celebrate the lessons, bury the pain, and step into the light of now. Your destiny is calling you. Step forward with faith, move with courage, and walk with the unshakable certainty that God goes before you, preparing the way. Every step you take toward your purpose is guided by His hand. Trust Him, embrace your calling, and move boldly into the future He has prepared for you. Your calling won't wait. Move forward with faith, courage, and confidence knowing God leads every step of the way.

Josh. 1:3,4 says, "Every place that the sole of your foot will tread upon I have given you." God has already taken care of where He is taking you, but you have to tread on it in order to get it. In other words, you have to seize your inheritance, the very thing that God has already prepared for you. The paths you walk, the doors you will enter, and the blessings you will inherit has already been prepared by God. Your inheritance is secure in Him. The promises are real, and the provision is ready. But there's a key principle you must understand. Blessings don't come to you while you sit idle. God's provision requires action on your part. The land is yours, but you must walk on it. The opportunities are there, but you must step into them. The inheritance is promised, but it becomes yours as you walk in faith toward it.

Tread boldly. Move in obedience. Step forward even when the path seems uncertain. Every step of faith positions you to receive what God has already set aside for you.

You're not earning your inheritance. He's already provided it, but you are to participate in bringing it into manifestation. Most men say they're waiting on God when the truth is God is waiting on them. God responds to motion. You can talk all you want but without action God will not respond. James 2:26 says, "Faith without works is dead." Whenever God did something significant in the life of a man in the Bible, it was after the man moved. God did not part the Red Sea until Moses held out the rod. Goliath did not fall until David ran toward him. If you have not yet reached your destiny, maybe it's because you haven't responded to what God wants you to do. If your feet are not moving in the direction God tells you to go, you will not see the supernatural in your life. Don't wait for everything to be perfect. Don't wait for fear to disappear. Your inheritance waits for your faith-filled steps. God has done His part. Now, walk in yours. Claim it. Possess it. Seize the fullness of His promise.

Focus on God, not people. Don't let people stop you from your progress. The children of Israel didn't enter the Promised Land because of people. They said, "There are giants there and we are as grasshoppers in their sight." They looked at their situation and let the size of the people dictate their action. Never allow people to have the final say in your life. David challenged Goliath because he wasn't going to let people interfere with God's plan. God is backing you up and He's bigger than all the giants in the land. Don't allow people with power, money, and prestige be kings over your life when you have your own King. Let the King of kings make the decisions in your life. A king who seeks to honor God knows that true strength, wisdom, and guidance come from the Almighty and not the applause or approval of men. While the crowd may cheer, the people may criticize, and the world may tempt with its fleeting opinions, a king's eyes must remain fixed on the One who sits on the eternal throne.

God alone is the source of discernment. God alone provides the courage to make hard decisions. God alone offers the peace that surpasses understanding. When a king chases the approval of men, he risks becoming a servant to human whims and losing sight of the divine mandate placed upon him. But when he turns fully to God, even the weightiest burdens become manageable, and his rule becomes righteous, just, and enduring. Let every king remember that the voice of the people is temporary, but the voice of God is eternal. The approval of God is the crown that never fades, the wisdom that never fails, and the legacy that lasts beyond generations. Focus on God, stand firm in His guidance, and let His will shape every decree, every action, and every decision. A king who walks with God may stand alone at times, but he will always stand in strength, honor, and divine favor. Keep moving. Don't let anyone's doubts block your dream. Your progress is louder than their words.

God has called you to a life of greatness and success - not by the standards of the world, but by His divine purpose. He has equipped you with gifts, vision, and destiny that are uniquely yours. Yet, true greatness is not achieved through ambition alone; it is anchored in obedience and intimacy with God. The path to success begins with being tied to God's Word. Just as a tree draws strength from its roots, your life draws strength, direction, and resilience from Scripture. When you meditate on His promises, walk in His principles, and allow His Word to guide every decision, your steps are ordered, and your path becomes sure. Greatness in God's kingdom is about character, faith, and perseverance. It is about aligning your dreams with His purpose and trusting that He will make your efforts fruitful. Success follows naturally when your life is rooted in the eternal truth of His Word because God blesses the work of the faithful. Your destiny is not just to succeed, but to shine as a testimony of God's glory.

| 12 |

"PSALM FOR A KING-PART 1

What is a king? He's a man who aligns his will with the will of God. He's a man who visibly demonstrates and follows the will of God under the Lordship of Jesus Christ in every area of his life. Without being aligned with the will of God, everything in your kingdom will be shaky and unsteady. Every man needs to know 1 Cor. 11:3 because it makes a profound statement about the concept of alignment. It says, "But I want you to know that the head of every man is Christ, the head of woman is man, and the head of Christ is God." This verse is saying there is an alignment for how life is supposed to work. God the Father is over Christ, Christ is over every Christian man, a man is over his wife. When you lose alignment, you lose covering. That's why Paul uses the word "head" in this verse. The word "head" refers to governing, guidance, covering, and responsibility. God takes responsibility for Christ, Christ takes responsibility for all Christian men, and a man takes responsibility for his wife.

A man of God is not defined by his strength, status, or success but by his submission to the Lordship of Jesus Christ. He walks in humility, knowing that his life is not his own but belongs to the One who redeemed him. In every decision, in every relationship, in every pursuit, he seeks to honor God's will above his own desires. He leads his home with love, serves others with compassion, and stands firm in truth even when the world wavers. His words reflect grace; his actions reveal integrity; his heart beats with obedience. He is not perfect, but he is surrendered to the will of God, allowing the Spirit of God to shape him daily into the image of Christ. Such a man doesn't just talk about faith, he lives it. His life becomes visible evidence of God's transforming power. Wherever he goes, people see Christ in him: in his discipline, in his character, and in his unwavering commitment to do the will of God. This is what it means to be a king, to be a man under authority, guided by purpose, and devoted to the King of kings.

A true man of God must model his life after Jesus who never acted on His own will or pursued His own agenda. He said, "I do nothing of Myself, but as My Father has taught Me, I speak these things" (John 8:28). His life was a continual expression of obedience, humility, and dependence on God's direction. To be like Jesus is to live in perfect agreement with the Father's purpose. It means surrendering pride, ambition, and personal plans so that the will of God can flow freely through one's life. Alignment with the Father produces authority, peace, and power. It brings clarity to decision-making and purity to motives. A man who walks in this divine alignment becomes a vessel of heaven on earth. His actions reflect God's heart, his words carry God's truth, and his presence brings God's peace. When a man chooses to live as Jesus lived - submitted, surrendered, and Spirit-led - he becomes the kind of man who moves mountains, restores families, and advances the Kingdom of God.

Be the man who walks in step with the Father. Let your heart beat in rhythm with His will, your thoughts align with His Word, and your life mirror the Son who showed us what perfect manhood truly looks like. What does an aligned life look like? Psalm 128 tells you. This psalm was written to men who want to be kings. It is a psalm for a king for it describes what the life of a king looks like when his life is aligned properly underneath God. It covers a king's personal life, his family life, his church life, and his community life. This psalm gives us a vision of godly success as it describes the man who fears the Lord and walks in His ways, a man whose relationship with God shapes his work, his home, his family, and his future. Psalm 128 is a short but powerful psalm that highlights the blessings of those who fear the Lord and walks in submission to His will and purpose. It promises that a life lived in obedience and reverence to God leads to happiness, prosperity, and peace.

As goes a king, so goes his kingdom. It's true, a kingdom is only as good as the king who rules over it. The character, wisdom, and integrity of the ruler determine the strength and stability of the realm. When a king walks in righteousness, his people dwell in peace; when he leads with justice, the land prospers. But when pride, corruption, or neglect take the throne, the kingdom begins to crumble from within. The heart of the king sets the tone for the hearts of his subjects. True greatness in any kingdom is not measured by its wealth or power, but by the moral and spiritual leadership of the one who reigns. The path to a better world begins with you. This is why your personal life is so important. Ps. 128:1,2 says, "How blessed is everyone who fears the Lord, who walks in His ways. When you eat the labor of your hands, you shall be happy, and it shall be well with you." The psalmist begins by pronouncing a blessing on kings who fear God.

To fear the Lord does not mean to live in terror or dread, but to live in reverence, awe, and deep respect for who He is. It means to honor Him above all else, to place His will before your own and to walk in obedience to His Word. This kind of fear is not crippling; it is liberating, because it sets your heart in proper alignment with God's truth. When you walk in that kind of reverence, you begin to make decisions that honor God, living with a deep awareness that God sees everything, knows everything, and that He deserves your total obedience. You turn from sin not just because you're afraid of punishment but because you love Him too much to grieve His heart. It's the attitude that says, "Lord, I want to please You in every area of my life." Fearing the Lord affects how you work, how you speak, how you treat your wife, how you raise your children, and how you conduct your business. It's the foundation on which every blessing stands.

When you fear the Lord, you acknowledge that He is God and that you depend on His wisdom rather than your own understanding. You trust His timing, His justice, and His love. And from that place of humble reverence, when you walk in His ways and align your will with His will, flows every true blessing in life - peace, favor, protection, prosperity, and joy that cannot be shaken. What is a blessing? A blessing is experiencing, enjoying, and extending the goodness of God in your life. The blessings of those who fear the Lord reach far beyond material things. They touch the soul, the family, and even generations to come. It's having the goodness of God coming to you so that it flows through you. God's kingdom grows when you use the goodness He gives you to bless others. Fearing God is the foundational principle of God working in your life. A home built on the fear of the Lord is filled with light and anchored in stability. A life lived in reverence to God bears fruit that remains.

What does it mean to fear God? It means to reverence God and dread offending Him. It's a wholesome dread of displeasing God. It's when you present your body to Him as a living sacrifice. It's when you give God all of you. To take God seriously means to relate to Him on His standard rather than making Him come down to yours. It's when you walk in His ways. The man who fears God will take time to find out what God's purpose is for his life. You reverence God when you say, "Not my will, but Your will be done." The best thing you can do is get up in the morning and start your day with a God-focus. Say to Him, "God, you are my King and I am your servant. I want to represent You in everything I do. Wherever I go, with everyone I interact with, I give you permission to rule my world. I will talk the talk and walk the walk-in reverential fear

of You." Fearing God opens up the treasure chest to the blessings God has for you.

Is. 33:6 says, "The fear of the Lord is His treasure." The fear
of God is the foundation of life that opens up the treasures
of God. It's the master key that unlocks all the doors of the
blessings of God. Every true blessing, every lasting success, and
every door of divine favor begins with a heart that honors and
reveres God above all else. When you walk in the fear of the
Lord, you position yourself under the covering of His presence, and that becomes the master key that unlocks every other
door in the Kingdom. The fear of the Lord opens the door to
wisdom for the one who fears God receives divine insight to
make right decisions. It opens the door to provision for those
who honor Him lack nothing good (Psalm 34:9). It opens the
door to protection for His angel encamps around those who
fear Him (Psalm 34:7). It opens the door to favor and blessing
for the fear of the Lord attracts the goodness of God into every
area of life.

When the fear of the Lord governs your heart, you hold the
master key that opens the storehouse of heaven. Every blessing, every breakthrough, and every promise of God is accessed
through that sacred key. When you build your life on the fear
of the Lord, you will stand on unshakable ground. Your roots
will go deep, your faith will grow strong, and the treasures
of heaven begin to pour forth. What gets blessed when you
fear God? Your fortune. Ps. 128:2 says you will "eat the labor
of your hands." That's your fortune, your productivity,
your work. Your feelings. Vs. 2, "You shall be happy." Your fu-

ture. Vs. 2, "It shall be well with you." If you'll take God seriously, He will look after your fortune, your feelings, and your future. Walk in such a way that you can experience His will for your life. If you put God first, you will discover Him working on your behalf and blessing you in ways you never imagined. God rewards those who honor Him. Put Him first and watch how He takes care of the rest.

Notice that God doesn't bless laziness. He blesses the labor of your hands. The blessing of God doesn't fall on the idle, it falls on those who work diligently, faithfully, and righteously. God's favor causes the work of your hands to prosper. When you work with dedication, persistence, and steadfast commitment, God sees the effort of your hands. He honors your labor, turning your hard work into a blessing. Whether in small tasks or great undertakings, your obedience and purposeful devotion invite His favor into your life. He turns ordinary effort into extraordinary results. When you honor God in your work, He makes what you do fruitful. "Happiness" and "well-being" in this verse are not shallow emotions; they're the peace and satisfaction that come from knowing that God is with you in what you do. You might not have everything the world defines as success, but when God's hand is on your work you'll always have enough, and it will always be well with you.

A man of God must first learn to be a king at home before he can ever rule anywhere else. True leadership doesn't begin in the spotlight; it begins in the secret places of the home. If a man cannot lead his family with love, wisdom, and integrity, he cannot expect to lead others with righteousness and authority. Being a king at home means taking responsibility for the spiritual climate of your house. It means praying over your wife and children, providing not just financially but emotionally and spiritually. It means ruling with compassion and not control; to be serving, not demanding. Before David ever sat on the throne of Israel, he was faithful in his father's field. Likewise, before a man can lead nations, churches, or businesses, he must first prove himself faithful in his own household. God measures a man's greatness not by his public success, but by his private faithfulness. When you rule your home with godly wisdom, love, and humility, heaven recognizes you as a true king in God's kingdom.

If you want to be a king among men, start at home. Be the priest, the protector, and the provider God called you to be. When you rule your home with godly wisdom, love, and humility, heaven recognizes you as a true king in God's Kingdom. The first people to know you take God seriously are those in your own house. If they don't know it, then it doesn't matter what anybody else thinks about it. You are to be a king at home first. In the beginning, God created Adam and Eve and together they were to have dominion over the earth, to rule the world with authority. God made man to be the leader of the home, but he is not to lead alone. This is why God said in Gen. 2:18, "I will make him a helper comparable to him." When a woman is left out of the kingdom equation, you limit or even cancel God's involvement with you. A wife is made by God to be a collaborator alongside her husband. The word "collaborate" means 'to work jointly on an activity, especially to produce or create something.'

When a wife does not lead alongside her husband, the meaning and purpose for marriage has been lost. God made woman different than man. They have certain qualities that men do not have. This is why Ps. 128:3 says, "Your wife shall be like a fruitful vine in the very heart of your house." When you fear God, your wife will flourish. A godly man brings stability and fruitfulness to his home. When the head of the house fears the Lord, the blessing flows down to the rest of the family. The wife is described as a fruitful vine. She is beautiful, productive, and life-giving. Vines cling to something strong for support; in the same way, a godly husband provides spiritual covering and stability for his home. It is man's responsibility to create the environment in which his wife can flourish like a fruitful vine. Spiritual change takes place as a king uses kingdom principles, with God at the top, to invest in his wife.

Your wife is a valuable asset to your marriage. Ask your wife's opinion with an open mind. She is critical to the decision-making process because of her intuition, her mind, her feelings, her thoughts, and her contributions. Her opinions matter deeply. Take the time to ask her perspective on important matters and listen to what she says with an open mind, without rushing to judgment. Valuing her input strengthens your relationship and shows that you honor her as your partner. As the king of your home, you are entrusted with the responsibility to make the final decisions. You are the head, called to lead with wisdom and authority. But true leadership is never exercised in isolation. Your wife is your partner, your confidant, and your equal in counsel. Never make a final decision without first seeking and valuing her insight. When you lead together, with mutual respect and understanding, your home thrives under the guidance of a united front. Don't forget, in marriage two become one.

Ps. 128:3 says, "Your children will be like olive plants all around your table." The children are called olive plants. They are symbols of peace, strength, and longevity. Notice it says olive plants, not olive trees. It takes fifteen years for an olive plant to mature and become an olive tree, but it produces fruit for generations. That's what happens when a home is built on godly principles: it produces lasting fruit. If you nurture the olive plant right, it will produce olives for hundreds of years. In the Garden of Gethsemane today, there are 2000-year-old olive trees still producing olives because their roots run deep. If you want your children to grow straight, you must walk straight before them. Children don't always do what you say, they do what they see you do. Your walk with God becomes the seed that shapes their destiny. That's why your presence must be felt in your home. Proclaim what Joshua said, "As for me and my house, we will serve the Lord" (Josh. 24:15).

Sad to say, the roots of children today don't run deep because there is no one overseeing them. Most fathers are not in the home setting the conscience, the value system, the rights and wrongs for the children. Families are being destroyed because kings aren't leading them. Concerning Abraham, the Lord said, "For I have chosen him, so that he will command his children and his household after him to keep the way of the Lord by doing what is right and just" (Gen. 18:19). How do you get your children to become like olive plants? Ps. 128:3 tells you,

"All around the table." In the Bible, the way a king leads his family is around the table. That's where you sit down with the family and the leader in you takes over. The table isn't just for eating, it's for leading. The table is the place where kings take charge. The table gives you dominion, the right to rule. All the family sits around the table. You turn off the radio. You turn off the TV. You put down your smart phones.

At the table you review the sermon from last Sunday reflecting on the message, discussing key takeaways, and applying God's Word to your lives that week. At the table, you don't just share a meal, you share guidance and provide disciplinary instructions. At the table, you provide gentle yet firm instructions, shaping their hearts and guiding their steps. The dinner table becomes a place of nourishment for both body and soul. It's where you provide spiritual leadership, personal leadership, directional leadership, practical leadership. At the table, you pray for each child, covering them in love and protection. It's at the table where you set the tone for your home. It's where you make clear who the head of the house is - not by force, but by example and faith. It's where you declare to your family, "God rules in our house." Every meal becomes more than nourishment; it becomes a moment to honor Him, teach His ways, and lead with love and authority.

| 13 |

"PSALM FOR A KING-PART 2"

When a king walks in alignment under God, his life becomes a channel of divine influence. The blessings, wisdom, and favor he receives do not remain confined to him alone; they ripple outward, touching his family, his community, and even the nations around him. True leadership begins in the secret place of obedience and intimacy with God, and its effects are felt far beyond the throne. A king in God's alignment carries authority that transforms everything he touches. What happens next is found in Ps. 128:5, "The Lord bless you out of Zion." In the Bible, the word "Zion" referred to God's holy dwelling place, that special place set aside for God's unique presence. Jerusalem is built on Mt. Zion and in the city was the temple where a father took his family to worship God. The word "Zion" today refers to the New Testament church. It's the dwelling place of God, the place of His presence and power. Every true blessing comes from His presence.

The church is more than a building or a gathering; it is the local manifestation of the Kingdom of God. Wherever the church stands, it represents God's values, upholds His laws, and demonstrates His expectations to the world. The church is called to be a living example of righteousness, justice, mercy, and truth - guiding, serving, and shining as a beacon of God's presence in every community. It is the local manifestation of the kingdom of God, demonstrating in the world the values, laws, and expectations of God. It is inconceivable in the Bible that a king would not have a meaningful relationship with God's place of worship. When you are part of something larger than yourself, you will get more out of your experience with God. The degree to which you are involved in the local church is the degree to which the blessings of God will flow not only into your own life, but into the lives of those under your care.

As a king, your involvement in the local church is critical. In God's kingdom, every man called to be a king carries responsibility - not just in his personal life, but in the communities where he lives and serves. Your role as a spiritual leader extends beyond your home or workplace; it extends into the local church the place where God's people gather to worship, grow in faith, and advance His purposes. As a king, your presence, participation, and influence in the church are vital. Your gifts, leadership, and dedication help strengthen the body, provide direction, and model the heart of a true servant-leader. Being actively involved in the church does more than bless others; it also shapes you. Through fellowship, service, and accountability, you are refined, challenged, and equipped to lead your family, your community, and your sphere of influence with wisdom, courage, and integrity.

A king who withdraws from God's people weakens not only himself but also the kingdom he has been called to impact. On the other hand, a king who invests in the local church amplifies God's kingdom, demonstrating in real, practical ways what it means to live under God's authority and walk in His purposes. Your crown is not just a symbol of honor; it is a responsibility. And one of the most important ways to exercise that responsibility is by being an active, engaged, and faithful member of your local church. The church brings heaven to the earth so that the earth has a vehicle for the power of God to be manifested. It's the place where believers can love (1 John 4:12) and encourage one another. At church believers stir up one another to love and do good works (Heb. 10:24), serve one another (Gal. 5:13), and instruct one another (Rom. 15:14). It's also the place where you honor one another (Rom. 12:10) and be kind and compassionate to one another (Eph. 4:32).

For these reasons church attendance, participation, and fellowship should be a regular part of a king's life. A king does not rule effectively in isolation. Regular attendance at church is not a mere obligation; it is a vital expression of devotion and a recognition that God's kingdom is larger than the individual. Each service is an opportunity to hear God's voice, to be strengthened in faith, and to receive guidance for the assignments God has placed before him. Absence weakens the connection; presence strengthens authority, wisdom, and spiritual discernment. True kings are not passive in their roles. They engage, they serve, and they contribute to the well-being of the kingdom. Participation in church - whether through service, giving, teaching, or prayer - demonstrates a king's commitment to God's purposes. A king who gives of his time, talent, and treasure aligns himself with God's will and gains influence not for personal gain, but for kingdom advancement.

No king rules alone and there is always strength in unity. The strength of a king is amplified by a council, advisors, and allies. Fellowship with other believers provides accountability, encouragement, and spiritual sharpening. It is in the bonds of brotherhood that a king finds support for his spiritual journey, correction when pride or error creeps in, and inspiration to continue pursuing God's plan. Kingdom kings are nourished and fortified by the community of faith. A king's life is disciplined, intentional, and aligned with God's principles. Regular church attendance, active participation, and meaningful fellowship are not optional - they are the means that sustains a king's authority and influence. As he connects consistently with God and His people, the king grows in wisdom, courage, and the ability to manifest God's kingdom on the earth. A king who does this regularly and embraces it steps fully into the power, purpose, and inheritance God has prepared for him.

Eph. 3:10 (NLT) says, "God's purpose in all this was to use the church to display His wisdom in its rich variety to all the unseen rulers and authorities in the heavenly places." In other words, God decides what He's going to do with His power by checking with the church first. The church is not merely a gathering of believers; it is the living display of God's wisdom to the spiritual realm. God created the church to be His instrument of revelation. Just as a jewel reflects light in many directions, the church reflects the wisdom of God in multiple ways: through worship, unity, service, love, and obedience. When believers walk in the Spirit, their lives become a testimony that even angels and spiritual powers can see and recognize. The church is God's masterpiece on display, a divine instrument designed to communicate His wisdom to all realms. Based on what the church does, God decides what He will do. This is why Satan wants to keep men disconnected from the church.

For sure, the kingdom of God needs men who are kings to be responsible leaders in the church, men who will lead, govern, and take responsibility for His house with wisdom, integrity, and strength. The Church today doesn't merely need attendees; it needs leaders, men of faith, vision, and courage who understand their divine role as spiritual kings under the authority of the King of kings. 1 Tim. 3:1 says, "If a man desires to be a leader in the church, he desires a good thing." There is something noble about a man who desires to serve God's people. The call to leadership in the church is not a pursuit of power, prestige, or position; it is a pursuit of purpose. Paul reminds Timothy that the desire itself is good, because it reflects a heart that longs to serve God and care for His house. However, while the desire is good, it must be matched with godly character. Leadership in the church is not about ambition, but about responsibility. It is not about being seen, but about being faithful.

The church needs men who desire to lead - not for recognition, but for righteousness; not to build their own name, but to lift up the name of Jesus. God honors the man who says, "Lord, use me for Your glory." That desire is a seed that, when watered with humility, integrity, and love, produces fruit that blesses the entire body of Christ. So if you feel that stirring inside - to teach, to serve, to lead - don't suppress it. Let God refine it. Let Him mold your heart until your desire aligns with His design. Because when a man desires to be a leader in the church, he truly desires a good thing, a thing that honors God and strengthens His kingdom. Now is the time for the kings of God to stand up. The Church is the embassy of His kingdom on earth, and it needs strong, steady, righteous leadership. God is looking for men who will not just attend church but build it. Men who will not just hear His Word but enforce it. Men who will not just believe in His kingdom but advance it.

Jesus is the Cornerstone of the Church (1 Peter 2:6) and we are "like living stones being built into a spiritual house to be a holy priesthood" (vs. 5). All men are to be bonded together by one God, with one love, for one purpose. Jesus taught the disciples to pray, "Our Father who is in heaven" (Matt. 6:9), not "My Father who is in heaven." At church you need to be part of a group of men who are committed to the development, responsibility, and accountability toward one another. Men go to church for the collective worship of God for who He is, for what He has done, and for what you are trusting Him to do. The church is where men use their gifts, talents, and skills for the furtherance of the kingdom. Men also go to church for discipleship, that developmental process of the local church that moves a person from spiritual immaturity to being grown up in the things of God. The goal of the church is to primarily disciple men because men are responsible for discipling their families.

Ps. 128:5 says, "And may you see the good of Jerusalem all the days of your life." Notice the progression of this psalm. It went from the individual, to his family, to the church, to the city, to the entire nation. When men take on their role as kings, the world becomes a better place as everything around them begins to align with heaven's order. A king carries responsibility - not for his own glory, but for the good of those under his care. He leads with wisdom, protects with courage, and provides with love. When men embrace this calling, families are strengthened, communities are restored, and righteousness begins to flow through society like a river. If they don't, society deteriorates and evil becomes the norm. Look what happened to Sodom and Gomorrah. Ten righteous men could not be found in these two cities, so God destroyed them both. The proof of a man's kingship is his influence, the impact he has on the world around him.

Without an impact, you are not part of God's kingdom. Kings don't blend in, they stand out and make a difference. They openly and publicly represent the fact that they have a King and they belong to His kingdom. A true king rules not by domination, but by service. He governs his heart first, bringing it under the authority of God, so that his leadership reflects divine justice and mercy. When men live this way, the light of God's kingdom shines through their lives. Children grow up with direction. Women flourish under godly covering. Nations prosper under the guidance of men who seek first the Kingdom of God. The world suffers when men abandon their posts. But when they stand up as priests and kings unto God, the chaos begins to settle, order is restored, and peace reigns. The world becomes a better place because the heart of the King of kings is being revealed through His sons. The world around you ought to feel the positive impact of godly men becoming kings.

No government program can or will fix the problems the world is now facing. Unless men become kings, the world will not survive. It's true, the state of a nation depends on the state of the men in it. God designed men to rule not through domination, but through divine responsibility. From the very beginning, man was created to take dominion, to cultivate, to protect, and to lead under the authority of heaven. When Adam failed to walk in that calling, the earth fell into chaos. Every generation since has suffered from the absence of true kings, from men who know who they are in God and who govern their lives, families, and communities according to His righteousness. Only when men take their rightful place as kings will the atmosphere of a home, city, and nation radically change. Our world is not dying from a lack of resources, intelligence, or technology - it is perishing from a lack of godly leadership.

In Jer. 29:7 God had special instructions for His people who were living in a pagan land. He told them to "seek the peace of the city where I have caused you to be carried away captive, and pray to the Lord for it; for in its peace, you will have peace." The Israelites were to make the city a better place because of their presence. They were called upon by God to be an integral part of improving the condition of the evil society they lived in. When men refuse to rise into kingship, evil fills the void. Homes crumble, societies lose their moral compass, and nations drift away from God's truth. But when men stand as kings and men of integrity, vision, courage, and compassion, the kingdom of God begins to manifest on earth again. Unless men rise to their rightful place as kings, the world will continue to unravel. But when men reclaim their God-given authority and responsibility, nations will find healing, families will be restored, and the earth will once again reflect the order of heaven.

We live in a world that is starving for true manhood, for men who will rise above comfort, passivity, and selfish ambition to become the kings they were created to be. God designed men to lead, to protect, to serve, and to shape the world with integrity and righteousness. But too many have abandoned their post. Too many have surrendered their strength to fear, sin, or distraction. This is the reason why the world is waiting for its kings to stand up. The world needs men to man up and become the kings they were called to be, men who will make the world a better place. Why? Because the actions, choices, and values of the king determine the quality of life for those around them. This is true in both their homes and the country they live in. Now is the time to man up - not with arrogance or domination, but with purpose and conviction. The world needs men who will stand for truth, lead their families in love, and carry the values of God's kingdom into every part of society.

All men are called to be kings, and all kings are called to be leaders. A leader is someone who knows the way, goes the way, and shows the way. A real leader is first a learner, someone who takes the time to know the way. Before they can guide others, they must seek wisdom, direction, and understanding from God. A leader studies the path ahead, prays for insight, and discerns what is right and true. But knowing the way is only the beginning. A leader must also go the way. They don't merely talk about what should be done; they do it. Their life becomes a living testimony of faith, obedience, and integrity. When challenges come, they don't retreat; they walk forward in trust, modeling perseverance and courage for those who follow. Finally, a leader shows the way. By their example, others learn how to walk the path of righteousness, how to handle adversity, and how to remain faithful to God's call. Their leadership inspires others to rise higher, believe deeper, and serve better.

Ezra 7:10 says, "For Ezra had set his heart to study the law of the Lord and to practice it, and to teach His statutes and ordinances in Israel." Being a leader first requires personal responsibility and then responsibility to those around you. Leading well involves loving well. It requires that you put others above yourself. Align yourself under God in such a way that you place the best interests of those within your realm as a priority in your life. So rise up and be a king among men. Take your place. Step into your destiny. When men take their rightful place as kings under the authority of the true King - Jesus Christ - the world becomes a better place. Families are restored, communities are strengthened, and the Kingdom of God advances on earth. It's time to man up. It's time to reign with grace, lead with courage, and live with purpose. The world is waiting for the kings to rise.

A king orders his life to function personally under the lordship of Jesus Christ. His thoughts, words, actions, and prayers all line up with the will of God. Doing this causes his influence to go beyond himself and even beyond his children's children. Ps. 128:6 says, "Yes, may you see your children's children. Peace be upon Israel." That refers to leaving a lasting legacy. This will happen if you'll consistently model responsibility, love, kindness, courage, and devotion to God. In essence, leadership is not about commanding people - it's about leading them by example. Jesus Himself embodied this truth. He knew the way to the Father, He went the way through the cross, and He showed the way for all who would follow Him. Lead as Christ led - through wisdom, action, and example - knowing the way, going the way, and showing the way. Let the words courage, determination, strength, perseverance, tenacity, hope, and character be associated with your name. You are a king! Fight and never give up!

| 14 |

"LET THE KINGS ARISE"

Where do you go to find a king in the kingdom of God? The first place to look is in the mirror. The day you accepted Jesus Christ as your Lord and Savior, He empowered you to be a king. John 1:12 says, "But as many as received Him, them gave He power to become the sons of God." The son of a King is a king also. There is a king in you. Royal blood is in your veins. Too often, we search for leadership, strength, and authority outside ourselves - hoping someone else will rise up and show us what the kingdom looks like. But God's design was never to make you a spectator in His kingdom; He made you a participant. When you were born again, He placed His royal Spirit within you. The same Spirit that raised Christ from the dead now lives in you, empowering you to rule and reign in life through Him. So, when you ask, "Where do I find a king?" - look no further than the reflection staring back at you. Look in the mirror. The king you're looking for is you - chosen, anointed, and appointed by God.

For as long as you are a child of God, born again by the washing away of your sins, you are a king. Sad to say, there has been a cultural shift in how the world views men. In today's world, men have been undervalued, underutilized, and underappreciated. One thing is clear. When men don't rise up to their created role as kings, families, churches, and nations will be in trouble and the culture will disintegrate. When men do not lead their families in righteousness, homes lose direction. Wives carry burdens they were never meant to bear, and children grow up without vision or structure. When men shrink back in the church, spiritual authority weakens, truth is diluted, and compromise creeps in. And when men abdicate their roles in society, nations drift into moral confusion, corruption, and decay. Now is the time for men to rise up and take their rightful, God-given place as kings with the right spirit, attitude, and action. It is time to stand up and show up. The world is waiting for the return of righteous kings.

The fall of cultures is not a political problem; it's a leadership problem. When men stop walking as kings under Christ the King, disorder rushes in to fill the void. The culture disintegrates because the pillars meant to uphold it have fallen asleep. But there is hope. God is calling men once again to take their rightful place, to stand as kings who serve, lead, protect, and build according to heaven's design. When men rise, families heal. When men lead with humility and strength, the church is revived. And when kingdom-minded men step into their God-given authority, nations are transformed. Every man has been called by God to be a king and to fulfill a role in His kingdom. A king shows up where he needs to be, even if he wants to be somewhere else. His plan and God's plan may not always be the same. A king always goes with the plan of God. Make room in your life for the will of God. You've been called to action. You're not to stand on the sidelines watching everyone else do the work.

Inside every man of God lies a king waiting to be awakened - a ruler designed to govern his life, his home, and his destiny according to heaven's order. God never created you to be passive, hesitant, or uncertain about who you are. He placed within you royal authority, divine purpose, and the courage to lead with righteousness. It's time to let the king in you arise. You are not called to shrink back in fear or live beneath your spiritual potential. The King of kings has placed His Spirit within you, and that makes you more than a mere servant - you are a son of the Most High, endowed with heavenly power and responsibility. Embrace your God-given calling. Step out of the shadows of doubt and into the light of purpose. You were born for influence, anointed to lead, and appointed to carry out the will of God in your sphere of authority. Let your decisions reflect divine wisdom, your actions display heavenly courage, and your words carry the weight of a king who speaks life and truth.

Also, as a king among men, you must leave passivity behind. Passivity has no place in the heart of a king. Nothing threatens his call more than that. Passivity robs a king of his crown; it dulls his discernment and drains his strength. It convinces him to wait when he should move, to watch when he should war, and to hope when he should act. A true king understands that he cannot afford to be idle. He knows that silence in the face of evil is agreement with it. A passive heart is a surrendered heart, not surrendered to God, but to fear, comfort, or complacency. In the kingdom of God, a man cannot rule if he refuses to engage. Adam's silence in the Garden was the first act of passivity, and it led to the fall of man. When the serpent spoke lies, Adam said nothing. He stood by while his authority was undermined and his wife was deceived. From that moment on, God's call to men has been to rise up and take their rightful place, to speak truth, to act in faith, and to lead with conviction.

Kings don't wait for change; they create it. They move with power, speaks with purpose, and acts with love. They don't hide from conflict; they confront it with wisdom and grace. They don't sit on their thrones in comfort; they rule from their knees in prayer. A king doesn't sit idly, hoping the world will shift in his favor. He doesn't wait for circumstances to improve or for others to pave the way. A true king sees what needs to be done and steps forward, boldly shaping the reality around him. Change is not a gift handed to the passive - it is the reward of vision, courage, and decisive action. Kings recognize opportunity where others see obstacles. They move with purpose, lead with conviction, and leave a legacy that transforms not only their own lives but the lives of all they influence. Rise up and shake off the spirit of passivity. Take hold of your authority. Lead your home, your church, your community, and your world with bold faith. Stand up and create the change only a king can bring.

As a king you are called upon to dream, declare, prepare, and be generous. One of the first things we learn about kings is that they dream. Every man called by God to lead must first learn to dream. Before you can ever walk in your destiny, you must be able to see it. God never calls a man to be ordinary, He calls him to see beyond what is, into what can be. Every king in God's kingdom must be a visionary, because vision is what gives direction, purpose, and strength to leadership. When God gives a dream, it is not just a picture of possibility; it is a glimpse of divine purpose. Your dream is the blueprint of the future God wants to build through you. Gen. 37:1-10 tells how Joseph dreamed a dream. Everything in his life changed after that. A man without a dream will live by default, reacting to life instead of directing it. But a man with a dream walks with intention. His faith fuels his journey, his hope sustains his heart, and his obedience shapes his destiny.

Every great move of God begins with a dream in the heart of a man who believes. Abraham dreamed of a nation. David dreamed of a temple. Nehemiah dreamed of rebuilding the walls. Jesus came declaring the dream of the Father - to have a kingdom on earth just as it is in heaven. To be a king in God's kingdom means to carry heaven's vision in your heart and to lead others toward it. It means dreaming God-sized dreams, not because of your ability, but because of your faith in His power. So, dream boldly. See what others can't see. Believe what others say is impossible. Because the dream in your spirit is the seed of the kingdom God wants to establish through your life. Prov. 29:18 says, "Where there is no vision, the people perish." No matter how old or young you are, God's plan is for you to engage in the supernatural realm and have a dream for the future. Every king needs something in the future they're looking forward to and preparing for.

Most men never reach their full potential because they lack vision and because they're not connected to the great King who can empower them to fulfill their dreams. Without vision, a man drifts. He wakes up, works hard, and goes to bed, yet never truly moves toward destiny. He may achieve success by the world's standards, but deep inside he knows something is missing - a sense of divine purpose, a reason that gives meaning to every effort. Vision doesn't come from ambition; it comes from connection. True vision flows from the heart of the King of kings who created you with a purpose in mind. When a man disconnects from God, he loses sight of who he is and what he's meant to become. He begins to live reactively instead of purposefully, settling for survival instead of significance. But when a man reconnects to the great King, everything changes. The fog lifts. Dreams once thought impossible begin to awaken again.

You must be connected to God and stay connected to Him. This is the only way to live a fruitful life, a life that overflows. Kings need to dream and connect with God so they can bear fruit that remains. As a king, you have a destiny to accomplish something great on the earth. You were never meant to live small. You were born to reign with vision, authority, and divine purpose. But that destiny can only be unlocked in the presence of the King. Connect with Him, seek His will, align with His word, and allow His Spirit to breathe fresh fire into your soul. Strength, wisdom, and courage will rise within you because the power of heaven has begun to flow through you. You now see life not as a struggle to endure, but as a mission to fulfill. When you walk with the King, you'll begin to see like the King, think like the King, and live like the King. And that's when your true potential will finally be revealed.

There are moments in life when God deposits something deep within your heart - a dream, a calling, a purpose, or a divine assignment. But too often, those God-given visions fade because they were never written down, never clarified, and never acted upon. In Hab. 2:2, God gave all kings a timeless principle when He said, "Write the vision and make it plain on tablets." Writing the vision is not just an act of obedience; it's an act of declaration and an act of faith. All kings declare their vision. Dare to dream big dreams and don't hesitate to talk about your dreams, to make your dreams known. Every morning when you get up you need to speak your dream. Speak it over your life. Speak it over your future. Speak what God says is true about you and your dream. Call God's dream to fulfillment in your life. Believe that God is able to do more exceedingly abundantly above what you ask or think or dream (Eph. 3:20).

What do kings dream about? They dream of increasing their kingdom. They dream of dominion. They dream of seeing their kingdom expand, their influence grow, and their territory flourish under their rule. They dream of a future different than today, a future shaped by the words of God. Dreams give you hope and inspiration and desire and longing. Dreams give you a forward focus and keep you looking to God for divine direction. A king's dream is never small because a king's heart reflects the heart of his Creator. God is the King of kings, and His desire has always been that His kingdom would fill the earth. When God places His Spirit within a man, that man begins to think like royalty. The dreams of kings are kingdom dreams. They envision their families walking in holiness, their communities reflecting God's glory, and their nations bowing before the throne of the true King. You are called to dream like a king. Let your vision stretch. Let your prayers expand. Let your faith reach further.

Kings prepare for Eccl. 5:3 says a dream comes through much activity. Every great dream demands movement, effort, and consistency. Dreams are not fulfilled by chance but by action. When you pray, plan, and persist, your dream begins to take shape. God gives the vision, but He expects you to put your hands to the work. Every step you take, every seed you sow, and every small act of obedience moves you closer to what He promised. Go beyond the talking and put action to your faith. Do something to bring about your dream's fulfillment. Take the next step, even if it's small. Be faithful in the work, and God will be faithful to bring the dream to pass. Talking about your dreams and destiny will not bring them to pass. At some point, you have to move from declaration to demonstration. That means faith that does not produce corresponding action is lifeless and powerless. True faith is active. It takes steps, makes plans, and moves forward even when the outcome is unseen.

Whatever your dream is, do something to bring it closer to fulfillment. God honors movement. When Peter stepped out of the boat, the water held him up because he acted on Jesus' word. When the woman with the issue of blood reached out to touch Jesus' garment, she was healed because she acted on what she believed. Your faith must have feet. It must be visible through your obedience and effort. Talk stirs hope but action releases results. So today, stop only talking about what you believe God will do and start doing something that shows you believe it. Prov. 16:9 says, "A man's heart plans his way, but the Lord directs his steps." Make plans and stick with those plans unless the Lord directs you to do otherwise. God always gives big dreams. God's dream for your life is bigger and greater than you can imagine. Your dream is waiting on your move. Step out in faith, and God will meet you there.

Problems come with small thinking. Men are not thinking big enough. This puts a limit on what God can do in and through you. Don't get stuck in the mud of small thinking. The problem is not that the dream is too big. The problem is most men aren't big enough on the inside to fulfill the big dream God has for them. You have to dream, and you have to prepare! Then you have to grow into your dream. What you're facing right now is meant to help you one day fulfill your destiny. Joseph had a dream, and he grew through the difficult circumstances that came his way. God was with Joseph, preparing him for the fulfillment of his dream that was to come. All during this time Joseph was growing into his dream and, when the time was right, he went from the prison to the palace in a single day. He grew in his capacity to deal with other people. He dealt with the higher ups of society in Potiphar's house, and he dealt with the outcasts and downtrodden in prison.

God was equipping him to be able to manage and lead the country of people at every level. All of his trials and hardships were preparing him for the dream God had for him. Likewise, every trial you face, every hardship you endure, and every tear you shed is not wasted in God's plan. The road to your dream is not always smooth, but it is always purposeful. God uses the very things that seem to break you to build you. He is shaping your character, refining your faith, and preparing your heart to carry the weight of the promise He has for you. Before Joseph ever wore the robe of royalty, he wore the chains of slavery. Before David ever sat on the throne, he hid in caves. Before Jesus ever rose in glory, He carried a cross. Preparation always comes before promotion. The pain you feel today is strengthening you for the purpose that lies ahead. So don't despise your process. Don't give up when the path feels hard or the dream feels distant. Hold on, stay faithful, and trust that God's timing is perfect.

God is using every challenge to mold you into the person capable of walking in His dream for your life. Your trials are not the end - they are the training ground for your destiny. When the moment comes, you'll look back and realize that every hardship was preparation for the greatness He planned all along. The trials Joseph faced is what caused him to develop and grow in godly character. He dealt with being hated by his brothers, being sold as a slave, and being falsely accused by Potiphar's wife. He had to face all these things. He had to go through God's training process for kings. When all was said and done, Joseph showed great grace and generosity to his brothers. He said, "God sent me beforehand. I'm here to provide for you." Grace and generosity. Those are qualities of a great character. True greatness is not measured by how much a person achieves or possesses, but by how they treat others along the way. All kings are called to be generous.

Grace and generosity are the twin marks of a heart shaped by God. Grace shows itself in how you respond to others' faults - with patience, forgiveness, and understanding rather than judgment or bitterness. Generosity shows itself in how you use what you have—our time, resources, and compassion - to lift others up rather than build ourselves higher. A gracious person reflects the nature of Christ, who, though He was perfect, extended mercy to the undeserving. A generous person mirrors the heart of the Father, who gives freely and abundantly without expecting anything in return. Together, grace and generosity reveal the beauty of a life that is rich in love and anchored in humility. When you walk in grace, you disarm conflict. When you walk in generosity, you change lives. And when both flow from your heart, you become an instrument of God's goodness in a world that desperately needs His touch.

Great character is not found in pride or power, it is found in those who give, forgive, and live with open hands and open hearts. Most men find it hard to be kind and gracious to people who have hurt them. They're too small to be great. They have to grow. Trials come to bring growth in kings. You have to grow and be strong to handle the kind of pressure kings face. Joseph was treated and chained like a scum but, through strength of character, he served and worked his way to the top. He was determined! He had internal strength and a godly character. In time everybody came to love Joseph, trust him, and believe in him. The word of the Lord came to pass. His dream was fulfilled. Character creates the foundation that lifts you higher and keeps you there. Through strength of character, you can rise to the top - one choice, one challenge, one act of integrity at a time. Gen. 49:22 (NIV) says, "Joseph is a fruitful vine, a fruitful vine near a spring whose branches climb over a wall."

The key to Joseph's success is that he had a well of life that came out of a close relationship with God. His branches climbed over a wall. In other words, he was always ready to be bigger. He could not be contained. Gen. 49:23 (NIV) says, "With bitterness the archers attacked him; they shot at him with hostility." The archers wounded him, but his strength remained. Vs. 24, "But his bow remained in strength, and the arms of his hands were made strong by the hands of the Mighty God of Jacob." His arms remained strong and his bow was strong. He didn't shoot the arrows of bitterness, he shot words of faith, words of blessing. In the midst of adversity, his strength remained because God strengthened him. His bow was strong. His bow was his mouth and his words were the arrows. From his bow came the words, "I will arise to fulfill my destiny! I will come into dominion! I will arise!' You are a king so live like one. Kings dream, kings declare, kings prepare, and kings are generous.

| 15 |

"MASCULINE ENERGY"

All men should have the desire to be the king God wants them to be, a man after His own heart, ruling not from a throne of pride but from a place of purpose, integrity, and spiritual strength. Every man is born with a divine calling to lead, to protect, to guide, and to reflect the heart of God in the world around him. Deep within the soul of every man lies a God-given desire to rule, not in pride or domination, but in righteousness and humility. This kingship is not about earthly crowns or worldly authority; it is about spiritual responsibility and divine purpose. God never created men to wander aimlessly or live without direction. He designed men to be kings under His ultimate kingship, to establish His order, His justice, and His love wherever they stand. A true king doesn't demand respect; he earns it through service. He doesn't seek power; he seeks God's presence. He doesn't build his own kingdom; he advances the kingdom of heaven.

The world needs men who will rise up, take their rightful place, and lead with faith, courage, and love. When a man surrenders his will to God, he becomes equipped to reign with wisdom and compassion. His leadership becomes a reflection of Christ - the King of kings - who led by example, who served, who sacrificed, and who loved unconditionally. For when men become the kings God designed them to be, families are strengthened, communities are restored, and the Kingdom of God advances on earth as it is in Heaven. To be a king you must have a king mindset and it starts with managing your masculine energy. That's what separates boys from men and men from kings. Today's generation has no clue how to manage themselves in a masculine fashion. Masculine energy is "do something" energy. It's not about how big your muscles are. It's about doing the right thing when it needs to be done. Kings confront problems, not run away from them.

True kings never sit idle. They are always looking for something to do in order to make this world a better place. They are never content doing nothing. They don't sit back and let others do the work for them. Kings understand that leadership is not a title, it's a calling. A king's heart is always searching for ways to bring light where there is darkness, order where there is chaos, and hope where there is despair. He wakes each day with a sense of purpose, knowing that his influence is meant to reflect the heart of God in the earth. Kings are builders. They see broken systems and dream of restoration. They see hurting people and move to bring healing. Their authority is not for domination but for transformation. A king's eyes are always scanning the horizon, looking for the next opportunity to serve, uplift, and make a difference. To be a king is to carry the heart of your Father: to seek peace, to establish righteousness, and to make the world better because you were in it.

In God's kingdom, every man is called to think and act like a king, someone entrusted with divine purpose and heavenly responsibility. They serve, they build, and they make the world a reflection of God's kingdom. They serve with masculine energy which is "take charge" energy. Kings are not passive. They don't sit on the sidelines while others take action and get the job done. Masculine energy is "leader" energy. Kings are leaders, not followers. Kings are not weak in their decision making and they don't crumble when under pressure. Kings are not lazy expecting others to take care of them. Those who are lazy lack ambition and have no goals in life. Masculine energy gives you confidence. People look up to and follow a king with confidence. Confidence is when you believe you can do what God tells you to do. With confidence there is no problem you won't face head-on. David had confidence and he ran toward the giant. Kings believe there is no such thing as failure, only lessons to be learned.

Every man must one day look deep within and ask himself, "Am I a servant or a king, a follower or a leader?" This question reaches beyond titles, positions, or power for it strikes at the heart of who you are in God's Kingdom. A servant understands humility, obedience, and love. He lays down his pride to lift others up. He follows the example of Jesus Christ, who came "not to be served, but to serve" (Mark 10:45). Yet within every true servant lies the heart of a king, one who rules not with an iron fist, but with righteousness, wisdom, and compassion.

When you ask yourself the question - "Am I a servant or a king, a follower or a leader? - the answer is you are called to be both. A king serves with humility and leads with love. He follows Christ so faithfully that others are inspired to faithfully follow him. Rule not for your own glory, but for His. For in the end, the greatest men are those who have learned to wear both the towel of the servant and the crown of the king.

Jesus said in John 15:15, "No longer do I call you servants, but I have called you friends." Friends of kings are usually kings also. In the kingdom of God, relationships are not casual - they are covenantal. When you walk with a king, you are walking in the company of greatness. The influence of royalty is contagious. Those who are close to kings learn their ways, adopt their values, and begin to carry themselves with the same authority and dignity. Scripture shows us this pattern over and over again. David's mighty men were not born mighty but became mighty because they walked with a king. Their association with David elevated them from ordinary men to warriors of renown. Likewise, those who walk closely with King Jesus, the King of kings, cannot remain common. His presence transforms servants into sons, and followers into rulers who reign in life through Him. If your company determines your character, then your fellowship with the King determines your destiny.

Stay close to the throne, and you will find that the fragrance of royalty begins to rest on you. You will think differently, speak differently, and act differently because the spirit of kingship will be upon you. You are known by the company you keep.

And if your closest friend is the King of kings, then kingship is already written into your identity. Walk boldly in that truth knowing you are royalty by association. You received the Holy Spirit when you got born again. The divine DNA of God is inside of you. Because of this, it is natural for you to connect with God, to walk and talk with Him. It's natural for you to speak and interact with Him, to follow in the things of the Spirit. You are in God's royal family, a family that knows how to serve one another and meet needs. In every generation, God has sought not servants who merely obey Him out of duty, but friends who walk with Him out of love. It's the friends of God who become kings of God.

Friendship with God is the highest calling of humanity, for it is born from intimacy, trust, and shared purpose. When a person becomes a friend of God, they begin to see through His eyes, feel with His heart, and move according to His will. It was friendship that lifted Abraham from being a man of faith to being called "the friend of God." It was friendship that made David not just a shepherd boy, but a king after God's own heart. And it was friendship that Jesus offered when He said, "I no longer call you servants, but friends" (John 15:15). Those who learn to walk with God as friends are entrusted with His authority. They rule not by force, but by love; not to dominate, but to bring heaven's order into the earth. When God finds a friend He can trust, He shares His dominion with them. So seek not the throne, but the friendship. Draw near to God in intimacy and obedience. For in the quiet place of communion, He crowns His friends with authority and makes them kings who reign with Him forever.

In John 13 Jesus modeled how a king acts when He took off His outer garments and washed the feet of the disciples. This is one of the most powerful and paradoxical moments in all of scripture. The King of kings rises from supper, removes His outer garments, wraps a towel around His waist, and kneels to wash the feet of His disciples. What a picture of divine humility! The One who spoke the universe into existence stoops to serve the dust of the earth. He knew that all authority in heaven and on earth had been given to Him, yet He used that authority not to exalt Himself, but to serve others. Jesus was showing us what true kingship looks like. A worldly king demands honor; Christ gave it. A worldly ruler seeks to be served; Christ became the servant. He revealed that greatness in the kingdom of God is measured not by position, but by the posture of a servant's heart. Kings are not servants, but they do serve. Kings serve by leading and lead by serving. A king is who you are, serving is what you do.

When Jesus knelt to wash the disciples' feet, He showed us a kingdom where kings serve. When He embraced lepers, listened to beggars, dined with sinners, and healed the powerless, He demonstrated that the highest authority is expressed through the deepest compassion. He never distanced Himself from human pain; He stepped into it. He never ignored the lowest levels of human need; He ministered at those very levels with love, power, and humility. When He took off His outer garments, He symbolically laid aside His glory to meet humanity at its lowest point. When He washed their feet, He cleansed not just the dirt of the road, but the pride that keeps people from love. Jesus taught us that the path to greatness runs downward - into the places others avoid, toward the people others overlook. When you minister to the lowest levels of life, you stand shoulder to shoulder with the One who came to seek and save the lost.

In God's kingdom, greatness is never measured by thrones, titles, or the applause of men - it is measured by how low one is willing to stoop to lift another up. Jesus embodied this truth perfectly. Though He is the King of kings, He walked among the forgotten, touched the untouchable, and dignified the broken. He revealed that in God's kingdom, true royalty does not rise above the needs of people, it descends into them. When He took off His outer garments, He symbolically laid aside His glory to meet humanity at its lowest point. When He washed their feet, He cleansed not just the dirt of the road, but the pride that keeps people from love. And then He said, "I have given you an example, that you should do as I have done to you" (John 13:15). The King who knelt calls us to follow His example - to lead by serving, to reign by humbling ourselves, and to love without measure. In the kingdom of God, crowns are worn by those willing to kneel.

A divine shift is taking place. God is taking you from being a slave to being a king. The wise men asked, "Where is He who has been born King of the Jews?" (Matt. 2:2). Jesus was born a King! You were too! Jesus did not come merely to announce the kingdom of God; He came to establish it. And in doing so, He became the first of a new kind of king - a king whose crown was humility, whose scepter was righteousness, and whose throne was the human heart. Jesus is the firstborn among many brethren, the first of many kings who would rise up in His likeness to advance God's kingdom on the earth. Your royalty and your part of an eternal kingdom that's going to go on forever. Once you know you're a king, you've got to think and act like a king. He sent the Holy Spirit to live inside of you, bringing with Him the DNA of God. You've been anointed with power and authority from on high. There is kingly seed inside of you. That being so, Jesus tells you to "go into all the world."

Jesus is launching you into the world where you'll have a global mission to advance the kingdom of God. Through His Spirit, He is calling all men into this same royal calling, to have the same heart as Jesus, a heart willing to wash feet, heal the broken, lift the fallen, and proclaim good news to the poor. Jesus is the pattern, the prototype, the model of the King God desires. And as you behold Him, you are transformed into His image, equipped to advance His kingdom everywhere your feet tread, everywhere your words speak life, everywhere your actions reveal His love. You are a king because He is King. You advance and go forward because He went before you, leading the way. You rule because He has given you His authority. Jesus, the first of many kings, invites you to rise up and lead like Him, love like Him, serve like Him, to bring God's kingdom into every corner of the world, to help make the lives of other people better.

Jesus showed His disciples how a kingly family is to behave. He showed them how kings act. Kings talk to one another. They meet and build friendships with one another. They understand the domain over which each one rules and they relate appropriately. Kings live out of a flow of revelation that comes from having a personal relationship with God. Kings hear from God directly. They don't let pastors or other ministers tell them what to do with their lives. Sermons may be helpful, but kings don't live by bread alone. They live by every word that God is personally speaking to them. Also, stop asking people to pray for you all the time. You're a king! Talk to God yourself! A king follows in the footsteps of Jesus. He was a King who knew how to wash feet. You're not a king sitting on a throne where people come and bow down to you. No, you're a king who gets on your knees so you can wash the dirty feet of others.

Slaves have a victim mentality. They say, "stuff happens" and accept whatever life throws at them. But kings are warriors! They're more than conquerors! Kings take charge and change the world they live in. A slave says, "Whatever will be, will be" but a king makes decrees and declarations. He changes things by the authority of his words. A servant waits for instructions; a king takes the initiative. God gave you a mind to think, design, imagine, create, and order your steps with. God gave you a mind so use it. To be a king, you must think like a king. Some men become Christians and they stop thinking. They get a slave mentality and wait to be told what to do. God never calls us to a position without giving us the mindset to carry it. Before a man ever walks in kingship, he must first learn to think like a king. Kings do not think in terms of defeat, fear, or limitation. They think in terms of purpose, responsibility, and divine authority.

A king understands that his thoughts shape his world. Scripture says, "As a man thinks in his heart, so is he" (Prov. 23:7). If you think small, you will live small. If you think defeated, you will walk in defeat. But if you think with the mind of Christ - boldly, righteously, and with heaven's perspective - you begin to rise into the authority God has given you. To be a king, you must think beyond the moment. Kings look ahead. They see the bigger picture. They steward vision, guard their territory, and protect what God has placed under their care. They make decisions based not on emotion, but on wisdom, courage, and God's Word. If you desire to walk in kingship, begin with your thoughts. Shape your mind according to God's truth. Think with purpose. Think with faith. Think with the confidence of one who knows he is chosen, appointed, and empowered by the King of kings. Before you ever rule, you must learn to think like the ruler God created you to be. You are called to be a king so start thinking like one.

Slaves bury their dreams and desires so they can be servants, people who are told what to do all the time. Kings have dreams, passions, and desires. They light a spiritual fire to what's inside of them and become energetic. Slaves wait to be told what to do. They don't rise up and take responsibility for what God has called them to do. Kings step out and believe the Holy Spirit will direct them as they go. A servant is passive, always waiting for instruction, whereas kings are proactive. A king takes the initiative and plans how he can advance his territory. A servant is so worried about getting it wrong and getting punished that he won't do anything until he gets an instruction. Kings know that risk and failure are part of the deal and they step out and go forward anyway. Servants live under the bondage of fear. Kings believe they can do all things through Christ which strengthens them.

A slave has a sense of entitlement. They think God owes them something. A king has a sense of responsibility. They think they owe something to God. A servant says, "What is God going to do for me?" A king says, "What can I do for God?" The servant with one talent buried it and didn't do anything. The other two made a profit and was commended and got promoted. A servant does nothing on his own while a king always has something to give and do. A servant values security and all he does is sit on a pew Sunday after Sunday. A king values destiny and he can never sit still on a pew for very long. He gets up and does all he can to advance the kingdom. Servants are always waiting for a revival. Kings go out and create one. Servants are so busy waiting they don't do anything. Kings remain busy with the talents God gave them. Kings grow and expand their giftings. They take the initiative and do things instead of waiting. Let the kings arise!

| 16 |

"ACT LIKE A KING"

Think about it. You are the offspring of a King! God's spiritual DNA is in you. Lift your head high for you are not ordinary! You are the offspring of the King of kings, born not of the will of man, but of God Himself (John 1:13). When you received Christ, you were adopted into the royal family of heaven. The blood that flows through your spiritual veins is royal blood - the blood of Jesus Christ, the Son of the living God. You were never meant to live defeated, fearful, or uncertain of your worth. Your Father sits upon the throne of glory, and as His child, you share in His inheritance. The world may see you as common, but heaven calls you chosen. You are a royal priesthood, a holy nation, set apart to show forth the praises of Him who called you out of darkness and into His marvelous light (1 Peter 2:9). God has chosen you so walk with confidence for your worth comes not from what you have, but from who your Father is.

You are a reflection of His glory, an ambassador of His kingdom, and a vessel of His divine nature. The same power that raised Christ from the dead lives in you. That means no situation, no struggle, and no storm can define or destroy who you are. Jesus is the King of kings. He is a King and He has many kings under His lordship. Stop seeing yourself as a wretched sinner in terms of your past or your failures. The Bible says, "Old things have passed away; behold, all things become new" (1 Cor. 5:17). Let go of the past and see yourself as a king under the kingship of Jesus Christ, called to advance His kingdom. Kings represent on the earth God's perspective from heaven. Their mission is to see that God's will gets done on earth just as it is in heaven. So straighten your crown and remember who you belong to. You are the son of the Most High God - a royal heir, destined to reign with Christ. Live like it. Speak like it. Pray like it. Love like it. Because you are the offspring of a King!

What is a king? A king is a man who has completely surrendered his life to God. His greatness is not found in earthly titles or possessions, but in his obedience to the King of kings. True kingship begins at the feet of Jesus in humility, submission, and devotion. From that place of surrender flows divine authority, wisdom, and strength. His power is not his own, but comes from above, enabling him to lead, protect, and serve according to God's will. A man fully yielded to God becomes unstoppable, for Heaven itself stands behind the one who rules under the guidance of the Almighty. A king is a man who knows God and walks with God. They always carry themselves in a noble way. Kings act in a different way than how ordinary men act. Why is that? Because they know who they are and how they're to operate on the earth. A king knows how to be gentle. He's a man who knows how to be meek and tender. He walks softly but carries a big stick.

A true king is not defined by a crown or a throne but by his ability to discern the times, weigh his words, and make decisions guided by wisdom and humility. He sees beyond the surface of things, perceiving purpose in every season and lesson in every challenge. Understanding gives him balance, patience, and insight to lead not only others but also himself. A king is a good steward of what God has entrusted to him. He values his time, knowing it is one of his most precious resources. He spends it intentionally building, learning, leading, and serving. He manages his resources with integrity, generosity, and foresight, realizing that everything in his possession ultimately belongs to the King of kings. A true king takes responsibility as he faces challenges with courage and stands firm in his duties. Whether in success or failure, he owns his actions and learns from them. And above all, a king is a man of self-control. He governs his thoughts, speech, and conduct under the authority of God's Word.

Kings dream of enlarging their territory. they rise up and take new ground for the kingdom of God. Kings walk in the fruit of the Spirit and has a spiritual perspective about everything. Kings hear God speak and they receive prophetic direction, insight, and revelation from Him. John 10:27 says, "My sheep hear My voice, and I know them, and they follow Me." True kings in God's Kingdom lead not by sight or opinion, but by the voice of the King of kings. God gives His kings prophetic direction, divine insight, and revelation for every decision and season. A king's authority is only as effective as his ability to hear and obey divine instruction. A king who listens to God does not move in haste but waits for heaven's instruction. In prayer, worship, and stillness, God reveals His plans, giving wisdom beyond human understanding. To reign effectively, develop a heart that hears. Every act of true dominion begins with a word from God. Listen, obey, and rise in the authority He has entrusted to you.

God said in Is. 43:19, "Behold, I will do a new thing, now it shall spring forth; Shall you not know it?" God always has new things to say. Don't live in past experiences but find out what God is saying now. Don't live in yesterday's memories or mistakes. God is speaking today so listen, obey, and step into the life He's calling you to right now. The past is a lesson; the present is your opportunity. A new thing requires new direction and new revelation. God is speaking and you have to position yourself to hear what He has to say. Jesus spoke things to His disciples that He didn't say to the crowd (Mark 4:34). It was the disciples who spent time alone with Jesus. Are you spending time alone with God in order to hear what He is saying during this season of your life? Jesus came to speak a message about a kingdom that was advanced through signs and wonders, a kingdom that brings hope to people. Your purpose as a king among men is to expand that kingdom.

God is always moving, always speaking, always revealing new things. He wants to give you fresh insights, new directions, and deeper truths. The question is not whether He has something to say but whether you are listening. Too often, we get comfortable with what we know, holding onto familiar patterns and past revelations. But God's voice is alive, dynamic, and constantly calling us into something new. Are you willing to quiet the noise, open your heart, and tune your spirit to hear what He is saying today? New doors, fresh revelations, and life-changing moments await those who listen. You can't live off past experiences. You need to hear new things for a new day. You need to be experiencing a new dimension of God. This comes by hearing God speak. It comes by you positioning yourself to let God speak to you. In the story of Mary and Martha, Mary sat at the feet of Jesus and heard directly firsthand from the Lord. You need to do the same.

If you are called to be a king under Jesus Christ, you cannot lead by your own understanding. True kingship requires hearing directly from the King of kings. Prophetic direction is God's voice guiding your decisions, your strategies, and your steps. It may come as a whisper, a conviction, or a revelation through His Word, but it always aligns with His purposes. A king who walks in God's guidance avoids traps, makes wise decisions, and advances the kingdom. Cultivate intimacy with Jesus through prayer, fasting, and listening. Be sensitive to His Spirit. Obey what He shows you, even when it doesn't make sense to others. Daily you need to be hearing from Him concerning what He wants you to do. There is a fresh vision that God wants to put in your heart. Live with an anticipation of new things God is about to do. Today is a new day and God is saying new things. It's a day when ordinary men rise up with the supernatural power of God at work in their lives. It's a day when men become kings.

A king's heart is always focused on his kingdom. He desires to govern wisely, ensuring justice, peace, and prosperity throughout his territory. At the same time, a true king is not content to remain small; he seeks to enlarge his influence, extend his reach, and see his kingdom flourish beyond its current borders. Leadership is not just about maintaining what is given, but about growing, expanding, and making a lasting impact. Jesus was a visionary, and He was continually thinking about how to take new territory. His vision was to take the gospel message into every nation on the earth. God is causing men to arise with the challenge of going to new territories, of taking more ground for the kingdom of God. True leadership in God's kingdom is not only about stewardship, but about expansion, about bringing God's purposes, provision, and presence into every corner of the territory He has called you to oversee.

Be prepared for God to call you to leave the familiar shores of comfort and security and step into the unknown. On the other side of fear, hesitation, and doubt lies new territory, ground that God has prepared for you to advance His kingdom. It is a place where your faith can grow stronger, your gifts can be fully realized, and your impact can extend further than ever before. Do not wait for perfect conditions; the boat is already there. Step in, row, and let the Spirit guide you. The water may be uncertain, but the One who calls you knows the way. Each wave is an opportunity to trust Him, and every stroke brings you closer to the mission He has ordained for your life. God is not asking you to cross over alone for He goes with you, and on the other side, blessings, purpose, and new assignments await. Your obedience today unlocks the advancement of His kingdom tomorrow. Get in the boat and cross over to the other side. Waiting for you is new territory to advance the kingdom in.

God's kingdom isn't meant to be observed from a distance; it's meant to break forth in your life. For that to happen you've got to move forward. Step out of passivity. Take that next step, speak that word of faith, obey that still small prompting in your heart. Every act of courage, every step of faith, aligns you with God's power and opens the door for His kingdom to manifest in ways you've never imagined. The breakthrough you've been waiting for won't come while you stand still. It comes when you move, when you trust, when you refuse to settle for the ordinary. God's kingdom is ready to flow through your life, but you have to position yourself to receive it. Your walk with God is a journey and you're to always be going forward. Paul said, "I press toward the goal for the prize of the upward call of God in Christ Jesus" (Phil. 3:14). Anyone who stays where they are has stopped going forward. They're dead in the water. Staying where you are is a horrible way to live. You need to be continually moving forward.

If you don't go forward, you'll miss what God is doing. Why? Because he is always doing a new thing. God is always moving. He is always creating, always calling, always orchestrating new things in the lives of His people. But if you refuse to move forward with Him, if you cling too tightly to the past, if you resist stepping out in faith, you will miss the blessings, the breakthroughs, and the new opportunities that He has prepared for you. God's ways are higher than our ways, and His timing is perfect. He is always doing a new thing - opening doors where there were walls, bringing hope where there was despair, and stretching our faith beyond what we ever imagined. But His blessings are not static. They require movement. They require obedience. They require faith in action. Stop standing still. Step out in faith. Break free from passivity and watch God's kingdom break forth in your life. Every step you take in obedience opens the door for His favor, breakthrough, and divine opportunities.

Don't wait! Move forward today! Expand your thinking. Don't limit God by what you see with your natural eyes. Dare to imagine what He can do in your life beyond your present circumstances. Expand your believing. Trust Him for more than you've experienced. Expect miracles. Walk in the confidence that God's plans for you are greater than anything you can plan for yourself. Expand your doing. Take steps of faith. Move when He nudges you. Act when He calls you. Respond when He stirs your heart. Follow God's gentle push and move in step with His guidance. Forward motion in obedience aligns you with God's unfolding plan. The moment you stop, the moment you hesitate, the moment you stop moving forward, is the moment God's "new thing" can pass by. Don't miss it. Don't get stuck in yesterday. Step forward and step into what He's already preparing. Trust Him. Stretch yourself because God is always moving, and His best for you is always ahead and never behind.

In the journey of faith, advancing into new territory often requires more than courage and vision - it requires discernment about who you allow to influence your path. To move forward, there will be seasons when you must walk away from those who, knowingly or unknowingly, hinder your progress. Even Jesus modeled this principle. Many times, He and His disciples left the crowds behind to go off by themselves to pray, to strategize, and to receive guidance from the Father. In those moments of solitude, they found clarity, renewed strength, and divine direction that enabled them to accomplish greater things. In solitude and in focused pursuit of God's will, you align with His power to claim what He has promised. Just as Jesus and His disciples advanced after withdrawing, so too will you find victory when you step away from distractions, hindrances, and negativity. Always remember that walking away is not rejection, it is preparation.

Don't follow the crowd and what everyone else is doing. Most of the time crowds are lost and bewildered, under all kinds of influence. Be like Jesus and leave the crowd behind. Choose wisely whom you walk with and be willing to walk alone when necessary. Your breakthrough, your new territory, and your divine assignment often await on the other side of that decisive step. It takes courage to stand apart when the world wants you to blend in. It takes courage to expand your territory, to step into places others fear, and to pursue the calling that is uniquely yours. And yes, it takes courage to resist the pressure of people and their opinions, expectations, and doubts. Be confident knowing every step you take outside the familiar, every choice to rise above conformity, strengthens your character and shapes your destiny. True growth comes when courage meets conviction. Dare to be different. Dare to go further.

Dare to stand firm, even when the world whispers, "Stay where you are."

Kings advance to new territory. They go forward and do what God is telling them to do. You can't go out into the seas of opportunity if you don't leave the shore of security. Sometimes you've got to step out and take risks, to do what others say can't be done. As you set out to advance your kingdom, opposition will come in the form of circumstances and people. The enemy will try to intimidate you and cause you to lose sight of your dream. He wants you to become full of fear and unbelief. Because of this you have to have a spiritual perspective so you'll be ready for the storms that will inevitably rise against you. New assignments bring new challenges. Keep your eyes on your assignment, not on the challenges. Don't look to what you're going through, look to where you're going to. God knows the end from the beginning. He gave you your assignment and He'll take you to its completion. You have to build your life on revelation and on the Word of God.

Kings have spiritual perspective so keep your eyes focused on God and His purpose for your life. Act like a king and not a victim. In a storm you need to rise up and assert your dominion. Be like Jesus who slept while a storm was raging around Him. He's a King and He acted like a King. He was sleeping and wasn't concerned about the circumstances. Why? He had a spiritual perspective. Not only that, He expected the disciples with Him to act like kings also. He expected them to stand up and speak to the storm and exercise kingly authority. He did what the disciples should have done. He spoke directly to the storm and told it to be quiet. Speak the Word of God into your storm. Tell the wind and the waves to be still. Kings decree, they don't beg! Stand up and speak strongly and firmly. Call those things that be not as though they were. That's how kings act. They speak over their lives and their circumstances. Kings take dominion over evil spirits. They declare that no weapon formed against them will prosper.

You need to rise up like a king and speak like a king. Why? Because you are a king! Stand in the authority God has given you, hold your head high and speak with the confidence of one who knows their destiny, for your words carry power and influence. When Jesus heard about the storm, He rose up! You also need to rise up and exercise your kingship. Speak to the enemy and frame your world according to the Word of God. Be like Caleb who said, "We are well able to take this land for God is with us." That's how a king speaks. You've got to act like a king, speak like a king, and frame your world like a king. Let go of what people think. Let go of your circumstances. Step out and do new things. When storms come, rise up and speak to it. Don't talk about your problems, talk to your problems. Keep your eyes fixed on what God told you to do. If He said to go to the other side, then believe no storm will stop you from getting there.

SUMMARY

Every man is born with divine purpose - a calling that reaches beyond the limits of ordinary life. God never created men to drift aimlessly or live-in defeat; He created them to rule with wisdom, walk in authority, and reflect His nature in the earth. To be a king in God's kingdom is not about earthly crowns or worldly power; it is about spiritual dominion, righteous leadership, and faithful stewardship over all that God entrusts to you.

As we've seen throughout this book, true kingship begins in the heart. It is established through submission to the King of kings - Jesus Christ. When a man yields his life to God's Word and allows the Holy Spirit to shape his character, he becomes a vessel of divine authority and influence. His words carry weight, his decisions bear fruit, and his presence brings order, peace, and blessing to those around him.

This calling is not reserved for a chosen few. Every man of faith has been anointed to lead in his sphere, in his home, his church, his workplace, and his community. The world may measure greatness by status or wealth, but the kingdom of God measures it by faithfulness, humility, and obedience to God's will.

Now is the time for men to rise up and take their rightful place as kings under God's rule. Stand firm in your identity. Walk boldly in your authority. Govern your life, your family, and your purpose with righteousness and compassion. The Kingdom of God needs men who will lead with courage, protect with integrity, and serve with love.

The crown you wear is not made of gold; it is forged in faith, refined through trials, and polished by obedience. So take your place, man of God. Rule well. Lead strong. And let your life declare to the world that the King still reigns through those who belong to Him.

You are called. You are chosen. You are a king in God's Kingdom. Now walk in your calling.

www.ingramcontent.com/pod-product-compliance
Lightning Source LLC
Chambersburg PA
CBHW070919130626
46555CB00001B/201